THE BARTENDER'S ENTERTAINMENT GUIDE©

1st Edition ~ 2011

Cover Design, Photography, Layout, Book Design, All Copy, Editing & Publishing

By Blake F. Donaldson ~ ~ ~ bfd Productions ~ ~ ~

Enjoy Any & All Alcoholic Beverages Safely & In Moderation.

Don't Drink & Drive

www.TheDrinkChef.com

Hermosa Beach,
California, USA
Blake@TheDrinkChef.com
Blake@BartendersEntertainmentGuide.com

ISBN-10: 0-9745059-4-3
ISBN-13: 978-0-9745059-4-7

Table of Contents

101 Cocktail Recipes

Chapter 5

Table of Contents

Bar Tricks — *Chapter 7*

Bar Pick-Up Lines — *Chapter 8*

Measures & Conversions — *Chapter 9*

Glossary of Terms — *Chapter 10*

Chapter 1
Bartending
101

This Book...

The contents of this guide are designed to give you, the perspective mixologist, a general idea of how to mix, shake, stir and pour some of the world's most popular cocktails and spirited beverages.
In addition, it will provide you with a wide range of other bar techniques designed to offer a lighthearted view into my world of bartending. These pages are by no means the final word on the matter, but rather a compendium of ideas and techniques to help steer you in the proper direction. Each 'spirit master' should utilize this book to enhance their own knowledge, confidence and creativity. Allow your own unique personality to emerge as you develop your own style and become the center of attention in any bar or social setting.

The following recipes, beginning on page 57, are for the most commonly called for drinks and cocktails, arranged in an easy-to-use, alphabetical reference format. Should one of your guests ask for a drink not listed here, ask them how to prepare it. They should know what they like to drink and what's in it. Plus, it can provide the opportunity for small talk and often help your guest to feel comfortable and involved. Don't be afraid to say, "I don't know that one." If they don't know either, ask them about what they like and offer something else they may enjoy. Be sincere and helpful and you will learn to master the situation.

The bar's a stage,

and the bartender is the leading role...

Okay...So You Wanna Be A Bartender?

What does it take to be a good bartender?

Confidence, sincerity and a little hard work.

That's it! The rest is mechanics, and that can be learned. The experience comes in time. The elusive thing is having the confidence to dazzle a birthday girl or guy and make them feel special, entertain a couple out on the town, flirt with a customer, or command the hearts of a rowdy band of reality challenged revelers. This book will equip you with some tools with which to accomplish this and to stand above the rest... to be the best. This book is designed to illustrate the subtle tricks of the trade for serious bartenders, players, playboys and entertainers out there in drink land. We will take this journey with one thing in mind, the essence of any good bar... Entertainment! It comes in many forms. Being a great bartender is one sure path to happy and entertained guests. Happy guests is what it's all about! You should welcome your guests like they were coming into your own home!

Of course, its not yours… Its your boss's business and they pay you to be there, welcoming his or her guests… Your guests. Its a great deal, It's your own little business. Of all you sell, you get at least 15% to 20% of each transaction. Push the food, sell the drinks… You get a cut of it all.

Don't get greedy. It all comes out in the end. 'Ring Everything Up'. Do your best to do your best.

The Culture of Bartending...

What is the culture of bartending?...
Forever I wondered too.
True professionals... are, or should be, protective of the art of bartending, cocktail pouring and the art of martini making in particular, coupled with the true sincerity of being a good host.
But each city has it's own 'culture' about how they pour drinks. If you go to London, They would never shake a martini... "It bruises the gin." It is to be stirred, gently. Well what is 'bruising the gin'? I asked a pro from across the pond... "It is an affront to the sensibilities of the gin. Nobody likes to be jostled about, perhaps caressed and slowly stirred, but never shaken."
Moreover the culture of bartending is a common state of mind of the participants in the profession of bartending. A pride and communal brotherhood, protecting the art of bartending. A sincerity to take care of your guests.
An unwavering pride that each of us protects and delights our guests, with the tools that we each have to work with. To follow the trends and fads of the day, more often than not, a passing fancy,
for some elixir or beverage of choice.
All the while preserving and protecting the style, grace and sincerity of a good bartender.
Do you mean it? Do you really think of yourself as the host of this party?

Well if you do... then you're ready... Go get em.

Your Personal Style...

So... If you want to develop a clientele, you have to have something to offer. Drinks are not enough. You must bring something to the table if you want them to remember you. It's easy to do, but you must set out to do it.

Most often your style will accommodate the place you find yourself working. But if you go in with a sincere desire to take care of your guests, you are already well on your way. If you're in a sports bar, well it's a natural that the best bartenders will be good bartenders and be well versed in the world of sports. If you are in a high-end place, as a bartender you will be knowledgeable about fine wines.

If you're in a blues joint... well you get the picture.

But a common thread to being a good bartender is to be sincere, always smile, even when you don't want to. Ask the guest about themselves, be interested. Scorn or a frown will never work to your advantage.

If nothing else... Keep 'em guessing.

The bar business can be quite frustrating at times. To be successful, you must mask this frustration. Never let 'em see you sweat.

So... styles. There are gamblers, magicians, sports guys or gals, tough chicks or bruiser guys, many are comedians. Buy yourself a joke book and you're in business.

Whatever your choice of style, be real and be educated. Don't go halfway with it. This book will help.

How Do I Get A Bartending Job?

How exactly do you get a bartending job?

They won't hire you without experience and you can't get experience if they wont hire you. The classic 'Catch 22.' What to do?

You've got to be smart, dedicated, flexible and be able to put up with some guff along the way. Bartenders can be a fierce lot. Wickedly protective of their coveted shifts. If you are a threat whatsoever, the other bartenders or bar manager will make your life difficult, to say the least.

Expect it! It will happen. The key is to brush it off and continue your game plan, to do a good job and create goodwill through hard work and attentive service. How do you get hired in the first place?

Make yourself available to the intended establishment by targeting the person in charge of hiring. Keep contacting this person until they hire you. Try to convince this person that you will be an asset. You will make their life easier. "Please, if you give me a chance… I will prove to you what I say, I will be early, work late, not complain, not steal, work hard and have a good attitude doing it all. If you hire me I will make you proud!" In all of this you must be sincere. Offer to do what the others won't do, like inventory, product stocking, cleaning projects, etc.

There's always something to do. Volunteer work, can work wonders.

Are All Those Stories True?

Yes, yes they are...and then some. Bartending can be as fun as it is lucrative. However, there are some pitfalls that must be negotiated properly in order to master your time as a bartender. Is this for everyone? Absolutely not. Is it a good starting position for someone trying to make some cash? Yes, it definitely can be. But generally, you will find that the true position of the bartender usually weeds out those not dedicated to it. Bartending has shown many people some of the wildest and craziest times of their lives. Things that give birth to spring break lore. Things that we don't tell Mom about. Should you decide to be a bartender...be forewarned. It's a fickle business with long, hard hours and temptation at every turn. The downside can be treacherous. The upside, however, can be both wonderful and profitable and your memories will last a lifetime.

The bartender ranks are made up of actors pretending to be bartenders...waiting to be actors.

The Origins

The origins of the 'cocktail' and the great 'era of the cocktail' show their roots in the end of the19th century.1872 in fact, shows the first patent application, by William Harnett, on the beginnings of what we know today as the cocktail shaker labeled an 'Apparatus for Mixing Drinks,' by the United States Patent Office.

The first mention, however, of spirited beverages goes back to ancient Egypt, many thousands of years ago, in hieroglyphics. 'Mead,' similar to beer, was very important to this and many other ancient civilizations, evident in the offerings to the gods in many an ancient tomb. Before this, one can only speculate how intertwined these various beverages were to the myriad of small bands of tribes scattered throughout the world, and throughout history.

The fermented beverage has always been an important part of most of the world's cultures. Certainly a food source, perhaps an escape from the toils of life...but also, perhaps, an elixir of love, bringing people together since pre-history. Maybe one main common thread, through all cultures is the spirited beverage, whether it be wine, beer or cocktail is that they all have strong roots in religion, medicine and healing arts, Whatever the local belief, countless religious offerings, gatherings, rituals and ceremonies through the ages have been blessed with the local beverage of choice. Many cities have sprouted because of their proximity to grains.

Wine, Beer & Fermentation

All Forms of consumable alcohol have their origins in the process of 'fermentation'. Whether they be wine, beer or spirits, all consumable alcohols must first begin with the fermentation process. A very simple process. Fermentation is the natural process of the decomposition of the mixture of the organic components of carbohydrates and yeast. (The Mash) The necessary ingredient in fermentation from these items is essentially carbohydrates.
Since carbohydrates and yeast are found in abundance in just about every sustainable society worldwide, almost every civilization has developed some type of alcoholic beverage early in their respective history. The fermentation process utilizes sugars that are hidden in the products used, which when mixed with yeast, create a reaction which then expels alcohol as a by-product. The base products used in this worldwide production range from rice to sugar cane, grapes, honey, assorted grains or even potatoes. All these organic products contain carbohydrates. Beer and Wine production use the process of fermentation and stop there with the desired end result. Each product exhibiting the characteristics of the base product used in it's creation. For example, malted barley, hops, yeast and raspberries, when fermented will yield a raspberry flavored beer. Wherever you are and whatever you use, will determine the local spirit.

Spirits & Distillation

Spirits, on the other hand, take this ‘alcoholic brew' or mash, and pass it through another process called ‘distillation'.

Distillation basically vaporizes the alcohol out and away from the water and mash that is the medium for the fermentation process. Remember here that a ‘fermented’ product already has alcohol in it as a by product of the process of fermentation.

‘Distillation' is then the process of heating this water and fermented alcoholic ‘brew' to the point where one of the products (alcohol) ‘boils' first, before the water and mash does. This is done in a heated and closed container called a ‘still'. There are many different kinds and styles of stills, however they all yield the intended elixir. The local’s choice. Alcohol boils at 173.3 degrees Fahrenheit and we all know that water boils at 212 degrees Fahrenheit, so if the master distiller keeps the brew or mash between these two temperatures, the steam from the alcohol rises and is collected in that curly collector tube that we have all seen in Hawk-Eye’s tent.

Spirits & Distillation

The tube is called a 'condenser' and as I said, the whole contraption is called a 'still'. The condensate that is derived from this process is the alcohol. It rises into the condenser, which is attached to the collector that, you guessed it, collects the vapor laden with alcohol. By the simple process of allowing this heated vapor to cool, it now changes back to a liquid. Presto...We have Vodka or Gin or Rum, or whatever product was intended depending on the original ingredients used to make it.

The process of distillation boils the fermented brew, which produces an alcoholic vapor that rises and is collected in the top of the still. This condensate is at a much higher concentration of alcohol than the original 'brew'.

This vapor is of course flavored by the original components of the original fermentation process.

All liquor is distilled clear. A good Whiskey, Scotch, Bourbon or Brandy gets it's color, and a lot of it's final flavor and character, from the casks that it aged in before being released for bottling.

Bar Tools Of The Trade

All bars need some tools. From the home bar to the high volume commercial operation, here are some tools of the trade...

Mixing Glass: A 16 oz. clear glass, with a heavy glass bottom. Often used as a beer glass called a 'pint'.

Boston Shaker Tin: A shiny silver open ended cup designed to go over the open end of the mixing glass to be used as a 'shaker'.

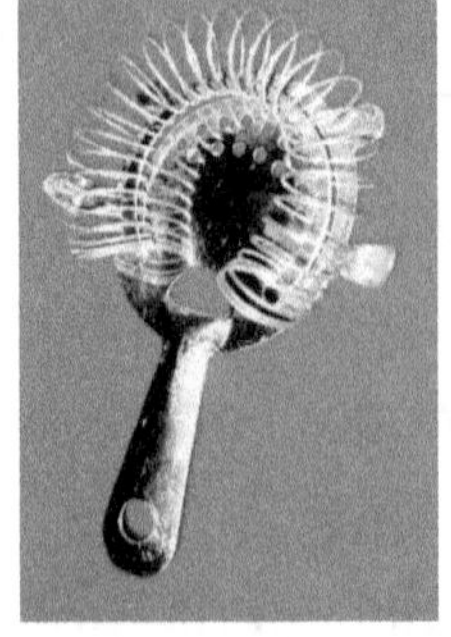

Strainer: Two sizes; one to be used with the shaker tin and one to be used with the mixing glass.

Chimney Shaker: A silver plated shaker tin with it's own removable lid and strainer.

Bar Tools Of The Trade

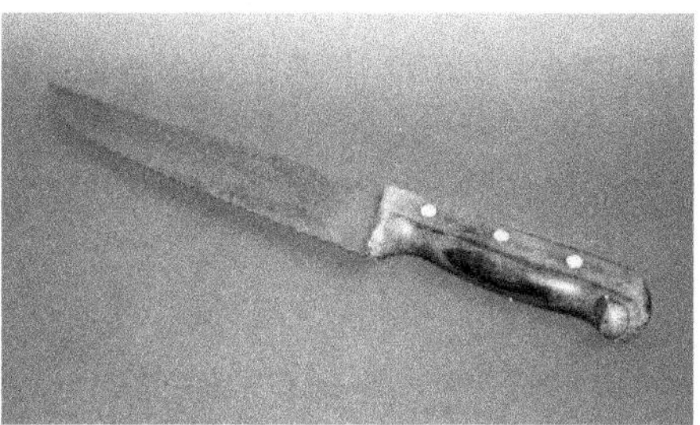

Knife: A serrated knife is fine and the safest, but I prefer a nice sharp boning knife. Be Careful!

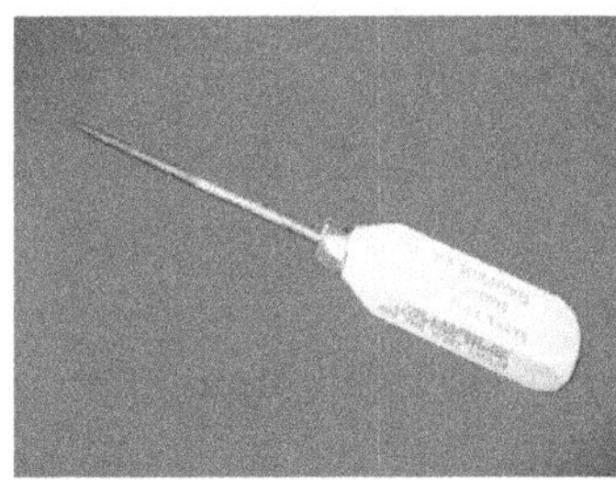

Ice Pick: You need this to make the correct citrus twists.

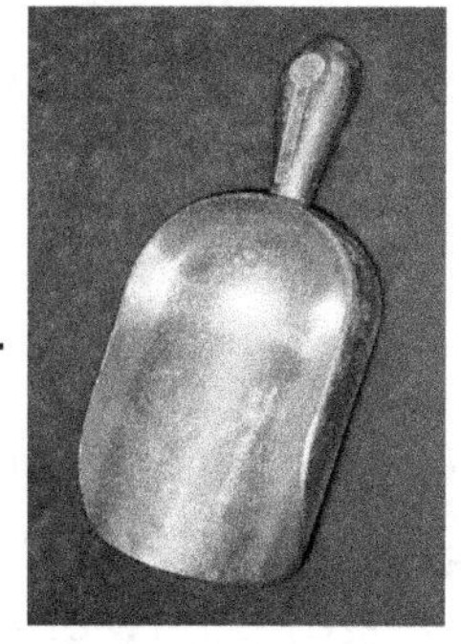

Ice Scoop: Most local health departments require the use of these. It is a very good idea to 'never' scoop ice with the serving glass. Never do it.

Glass Rimmer: This is used to moisten the rim of the serving glass with the sponge then it's dipped into salt or sugar.

Bar Tools Of The Trade

You will need to have these things on hand before you begin. There's nothing worse than an unprepared bartender.

Wine Key: Your most valuable tool. I prefer one with a long serrated blade. There are many different designs. This one is called a waiter's friend.

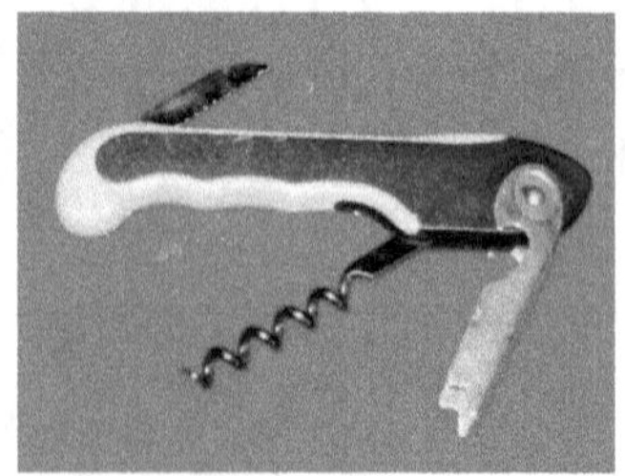

Muddler: Looks like a cut-off broom handle. Used to mash the fruit and flavors at the bottom of the mixing glass.

Lighter: For lighting birthday candles and cigarettes. It should be in your pocket every shift!

Jigger: This is used to pour liquor into and measure the amount used in the drink. Each side is a different measurement for different drinks and they come in varied sizes.

Bar Tools Of The Trade

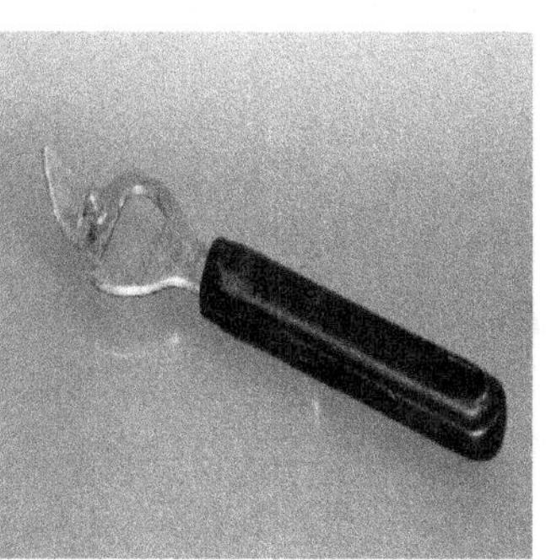

Beer Bottle / Can Opener: A bartender must have a proper bottle opener. Often called a 'church key'. Also, you need to have something to open cans. The pointy handheld unit is fine. Imagine that you need bloody mary mix on the fly.

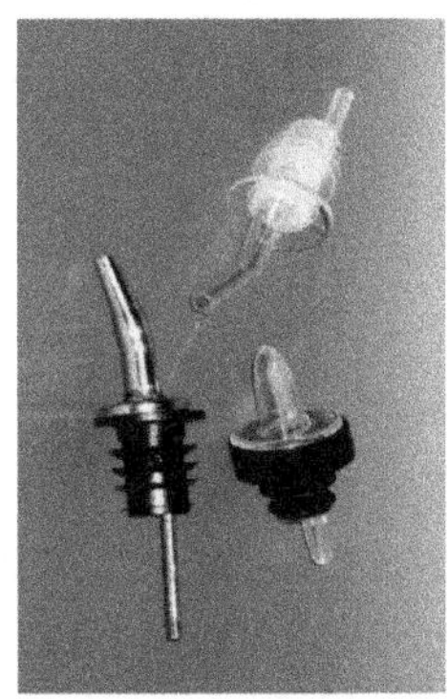

Pour Spouts: Or 'speed pourers'. They help direct the liquor and time the rate of the pour. They come in many different styles, designs and pour rates.

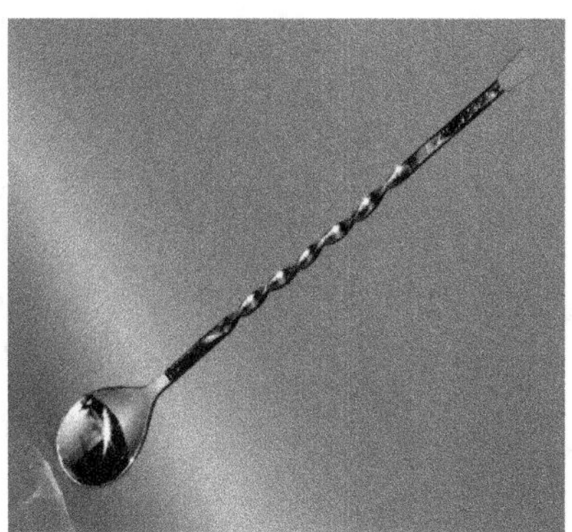

Bar Spoon: This is a handy unit. To help stir a martini, or layer a drink. The handle is twisted so you can roll it between your palms to create a mini blender.

Bartender Terms & Techniques

All drinks begin with the glassware. Some you will mix in a mixing glass and then pour into the final presentation glass. Others you will build directly into the serving glass. Listed below are some of the main techniques from bartenders from around the world.

Pour: Preferably with a pour spout on the bottle… One, One Thousand, Two, One Thousand, Three! (Count Fast). That is approximately 1 1/2 ounces of spirit. Adjust your timing to accommodate for the recipes that follow.

Build: Pour your ingredients in the order listed, over the ice in the glassware listed.

Blended or Frozen: Begin with a mixing glass. Pour all ingredients over ice into this. Then pour into a blender cup and blend until smooth.

Layer: Pour very slowly, either over a cherry held in your hand or a spoon, to deflect the turbulence caused by pouring. Begin with the thickest liqueur, finish with the lightest. 'Layering' will cause a cool visual effect.

Shake: Pour all ingredients over ice in a mixing glass. Top with a 'mixing tin' cup and shake vigorously. Try to leave some ice chips in there, but strain the ice cubes.

Strain: Put a 'strainer' over the mixing glass and 'strain' into your final glassware.

Bartender Terms & Techniques

Every bartender has their own style. Some are comfortable pouring into a mixing glass, others build drinks into the shaker tin. There are as many different styles and techniques as there are proud bartenders. Here is a list of some of the main drink presentations.

Rocks: This term refers to having the cocktail or liquor over ice.

Over: Means the same as 'Rocks.' Meaning 'Over' the ice.

Up: This refers to the pre-chilling and serving in an 'UP' martini glass. Served ice cold but without ice.

Tall: A drink or cocktail served in a 'Highball' glass, always with ice or 'Rocks.'

Neat: Served in a 'Rocks Glass' or an 'Old Fashioned Glass'. This term refers to the straight liquor served directly into the glass, nothing else. No Ice!

Bucket: This term refers to the preference of some patrons to have this slightly larger kind of 'Bucket Glass,' always served with 'ice' or 'rocks.'

Snifter: A globe shaped glass designed to concentrate the aromas of the liquor.

Common Bar Glassware

Common Bar Glassware

White Wine

Red Wine

Champagne Flute

Margarita

Champagne Saucer

Coffee Glass

Pilsner

Beer Mug

Chapter 2
Spirits

Vodka

There is much speculation as to the true origin of Vodka. The Russians and the Polish peoples both lay claim to this luxury liquor. Both of these countries claim the invention of vodka. Where it originated we do not know for sure. What we do know, is that almost simultaneously… the two countries, both… contributed to what vodka is today. In North Eastern Europe as early as the 14th century, 'Voda' is in many Slavic languages 'for dear little water'.

At or around the fifteenth century, this became the beverage of choice of the 'Great Czars' in the great lands of the Russian Republic… There came to be an affinity to this most neutral of all spirits, Vodka… or perhaps derived from the notion 'water' or 'Voda' of life. L'eau de Vie in French, it is not without friends. In the US it was virtually unknown through the 1930s. Not until after world war II did American consumers take hold of this chameleon of products. A virtually colorless, odorless and almost tasteless alcoholic beverage distilled from fermented wheat, rye, potatoes, corn or other grain products. Primarily wheat and corn. In history, potatoes were the carbohydrate of choice for Vodka, this vegetable was what was in abundance…

but now, grains and corn are cheaper and potatoes are more difficult to harvest.

So… you begin with a carbohydrate… mash to a pulp, add yeast and Presto… Alcohol and Co2. The Co2 is allowed to escape, leaving an alcoholic 'brew', often called the 'mash' or 'must'. This 'brew' is then filtered and distilled.

The distillation process removes impurities with each passing, prompting many vodka companies to 'premium distill' and 'specially filter' their vodkas over and over again for the smoothest taste. Some a half dozen times. To the point where they must add water back in to come within the legal limit of alcoholic content.

The filtration processes are varied as well. Some using diatomaceous earth, carbon or charcoal filtering is common even diamond dust… All in the pursuit of the cleanest yet tastiest Vodka of all. There are many… some 400 to this day. The neutral character of this spirit lends itself to the flavor of many, many mixers. The highest mixability rating of all spirits. It is no wonder the resurgence of popularity of this spirit. Vodka is the fastest growing category of all.

Gin

Gin is a clear alcoholic beverage distilled from grain, with certain 'botanicals' mixed in the brew before fermentation. Most predominant of these are the juniper berries which give this spirit its distinctive taste and aroma, also and often brewed with other herbs, spices and fruits like... lemon, coriander, licorice, anise, bitter almonds and orange peel. The exact mixture of these and many more ingredients is a closely guarded secret of each 'Gin House'. Their proud heritage is contained within the secret recipe, unique to each respective house. Aged in barrels, Gin is of Dutch origin. Genever is Dutch for Juniper, (genevier in French). Administered by monks of the 12th century to Bubonic Plague victims as a medicine, Gin was later used by 16th century doctors to treat kidney ailments. Revered by English soldiers as 'Dutch Courage', Gin soon began to gain popularity in England, much because of the well used shipping lanes in and around Europe in the 14th, 15th and 16th centuries. By the late 1700s Gin was the national drink of Britain.

This was attractive at the time because France, (The Enemy), was placing intolerably high taxes on their wine and brandy... So the British Government allowed any person who applied to the 'Excise Bureau' to set up their on distillery in order to avoid French taxes. Well before long, 20% of all English households were brewing their own Gin. The term 'Genevere' was shortened to 'Gin' at this time. The term 'bathtub gin' comes from the fact that this was the biggest vessel in the house so almost all home brewers were utilizing this vessel somewhere in their home production... That was before regulation and taxation took hold of this spirit. By the late 1800s this was the cocktail of choice among travelers to exotic places infested with mosquitoes, because of the tonic in the 'Gin & Tonic,' it was a popular thought at the time that the quinine of the tonic helped to ward off Malaria and the gin made the quinine taste better. Today Gin is the true choice of a traditionalist's 'Dry Martini' and still the 'Gin & Tonic' reigns true to this day. Alas… For so few producers, so fine an elixir...

Rum

An alcoholic beverage distilled from fermented sugar, sugar cane, cane syrup or molasses. Often blended to offer a special aroma, flavor or color and always determined by the master distiller. The slower the distillation process, the more sweet and full the rum will become. Rum comes from Caribbean origins and is aged in barrels. The longer the stay on the oak, the greater intensity, complexity and mellowing of the rum. The history of Rum is the history of sugar. Sugar is a sweet crystalline carbohydrate that occurs naturally in a variety of plants. One of those is the sugar cane, a tall, thick grass that has its origins in the islands of present-day Indonesia in the East Indies. Chinese traders spread its cultivation to Asia and on to India. Arabs in turn brought it to the Middle East and North Africa where it came to the attention of Europeans during the Crusades in the 11th century. As the Spanish and Portuguese began to venture out into the Atlantic Ocean, they planted sugar cane in the Canary and Azore Islands. In 1493 Christopher Columbus picked up cane cuttings from the Canaries while on his second voyage to the Americas and transplanted them to Hispaniola, as did Portuguese explorers in Brazil. Hispanola is an island in the Caribbean.

The Caribbean basin proved to have an ideal climate for growing sugar cane, and sugar production quickly spread around the islands. The insatiable demand in Europe for sugar soon led to the establishment of hundreds of sugar cane plantations and mills in the various English, Spanish, French, Portuguese, and Dutch colonies. These mills crushed the harvested cane and extracted the juice. Boiling this juice caused chunks of crystallized sugar to form. The remaining un-solidified juice was called melazas, from 'miel' the Spanish word for honey; in English this became molasses. Molasses is a sticky syrup that still contains a significant amount of sugar. Sugar mill operators soon noticed that when it was mixed with water and left out in the sun it would ferment naturally. Rum is made by distilling fermented sugar and water. This sugar comes from the sugar cane and is fermented from cane juice, concentrated cane juice, or molasses. Molasses is the sweet, sticky residue that remains after sugar cane juice is boiled and the crystallized sugar is extracted. Most Rum is made from molasses. Molasses is over 50% sugar, but it also contains significant amounts of minerals and other trace elements, which can contribute to the final flavor.

Tequila

Tequila is a finely crafted spirit of fermented juices obtained from the hearts of blue agave plants grown in the Tequila Region of Mexico. The liquor gets its name from the town of Tequila located in the state of Jalisco where production started more than 200 years ago. Agave is not a cactus, but can still take 12 to 14 years to mature. (Many producers rush this to 9 years or less). Tequila is made, slowly, from the distillation of fermented Agave 'heart' of the agave plant. The most sought after species of the many Agave is called the 'Tequilana Weber' or 'Blue Agave' variety. The silvery blue leaves and flavorful heart found on this plant yield a distinctive characteristic flavor, which distinguishes it from other agaves. The agave is allowed to be grown in only five Mexican states: Jalisco; Guanajuato; Michoacan; Nayarit and Tamaulipas. The spirit is only allowed to be produced in its town of origin. It is closely regulated by the Mexican government as well as a fiercely proud heritage of traditional production.

All tequila is distilled crystal clear or **'White'** also known as **'Silver'** or in country… **'Blanco.'**
This tequila goes directly into the bottle for sale.

Reposado is Tequila that has been aged from two months up to one year. Obviously a little darker in color than the silver, but not quite as dark as añejo.

Añejo is a term designating the tequila to be aged at least three years, usually in small oak barrels.

The language of tequila can be very confusing. To begin with, Tequila is the name of the town where production originally began, and it is also the name of the volcano overlooking this town. Locals in the Tequila Region refer to the blue agave plant as "mescal," and the fields where this plant is harvested are known as "mezcaleras." Many distillers call the distilled liquor mezcal but it is only called tequila after it is finally bottled. Before tequila became known as it is today, it was once called "vino mezcal" or mezcal wine. Mescal is a spirit derived from another species of the Agave plant, though produced in a similar fashion, Mescal is different than Tequila, though often confused as the same.

Scotch Whisky

A whisky distilled in Scotland from fermented local malted (germinated) barley and local grains that have been dried in a kiln over a 'peat' fire. This gives that particular batch a unique, rich and peaty flavor that carries into the bottle. The batch is then stored in oak casks, specially selected to target the master distiller's idea of the perfect scotch. Some proud houses use only one single strain of oak casks. Some reuse casks from products such as port or madeira. Some houses use both. In any event...

There are basically two kinds of 'Scotch Whisky:'

1. Malt Scotch Whisky, marketed as 'Single Malt Scotch.'
2. Blended Scotch Whisky, the majority of all Scotch lies her; A blend of Malt and Grain Scotches.

There are **Five Geographic Regions** in Scotland where Scotch Whisky is produced; Each region being madly passionate about their particular brew.

1. Lowlands
2. Islay (Island)
3. Campbletown
4. Highlands
5. Speyside

All Scotches are aged in oak barrels first… the distillate that comes from the distillery is called 'Plain British Spirits.' Not until at least three years on the oak, (usually much longer), can it be called 'Scotch Whisky.' Each producer has their own agenda. Often the casks used to age the scotch have been formerly employed as a sherry, port or bourbon cask.. Although aging is a critical component of the overall process of making fine Scotch, 'Where?' is the all important question. Where are the products from and where is it distilled? *Blended* Scotches comprise 95% of the North American market, however 'Single Malt Scotch' has been a very popular and growing trend in Scotch Whisky aficionados. To be labeled a 'Single Malt' it must be distilled in a single batch at the same distillery using select 'malted' barley. All must by law use the 'malted barley' as the main ingredient, the difference of each distinctive spirit arises out of the differences of local climate, the water and the peat used to dry the barley in a kiln. All these factors help by exposing their character in the flavor of the Scotch. The complexity of this fine spirit is delightful! Yes... It's spelled correctly. Scotland & sometimes Canada & Ireland use no 'e' in the spelling of their whisky.

Irish Whiskey

Irish Whisk(e)y is commonly believed to be a potato whiskey. This is not true. The misconception comes from the fact that the Irish themselves called their earliest, (and illicitly), distilled Whiskey 'Poteen' Whiskey. This term refers to the fact that they were first using a 'Pot Still.' This traditional distilling practice was the production of choice in its early stages. Whiskey in Ireland is distilled from the fermented grains, most commonly, 'barley,' usually malted barley, then un-malted barley, corn, rye, wheat and oats. The recipe is quite similar to the one used in Scotland, however, the proud difference being, where the produce is farmed as well as the water and the unique distillation process also has a tremendous effect on the distinctive flavor of the end product. The similarity to Scottish Whisky lies in the 'still process.' Irish Whiskey uses three distinct distilling operations. The first two mostly mirror Scottish distillation process; the difference is in the third. This is why Irish Whiskey is always 'triple distilled.' In each 'run through' of a still, the resulting liquid is of varying strength producing the distinctive recipe and flavor of this fine elixir.

Canadian Whiskey

Canadian Whiskey is often mistakenly called Rye Whiskey because it was originally based on Rye, but no more. The distinction of Canadian Whiskeys is that each master distiller uses the straight distillations of each respective grain… rye, barley and corn mostly, and blends these distillates together in a secret recipe to achieve a pure light spirit. Each master uses differing product ratios and different processes to obtain 'their' blend, distilled at least twice and aged commonly for four to six years in new casks of oak or even used casks that once contained Sherry, Bourbon or Brandy. Three years being minimum cave time, some producers blend their whiskeys before barrel aging and some wait until each whiskey has matured individually before they blend. In either event, the end result is a fine, easy drinking, mellow spirit.

Canadian Whiskey is made with a combination of corn, rye and barley. The blending of these grains delivers Canada its distinctive liquor. These cereals are mashed, fermented and distilled, yielding a light bodied, slightly pale and mellow flavored Whiskey. All major Canadian Whiskey producers offer primarily 'blended' Whiskeys.

American Whiskey

No matter where they come from, Whiskey is defined as the distillation of fermented grains, which are then stored in wooden casks to impart flavors, character, color and depth to an already fine spirit. The word Whiskey comes from the ancient Celtic word 'uisgebeatha' (Scottish) or 'uisgebaugh' (Irish), pronounced "wis-geh-baw". It is easy to see how Whiskey was to be called after these origins. Both cultures claim the first origins of this fine spirit, however this is an argument to be held forever, being that the ancients were enjoying Whiskey long before they were concerned with writing down the recipe for it. We will never know for sure.
American Whiskey began quite late in the day of recent history. The first distilled spirits commercially produced in the new colonies were Rums, first found in abundance in our young nation in New England. The beginnings of Whiskey being produced 'en masse' was not until early in the 18th century. Early settlers at that time were primarily using Rye and Barley for Whiskey production.

Preceding this production of course would be the inevitable taxes. In 1791, the new government of the colonies was in dying need, (literally), for cash to support itself. So… the excise tax on whiskey was born. Being that most early producers of Whiskey were homegrown outfits or small family businesses, they were adamantly against these taxes to the point of insurrection, riots and other nasty scenes. Well, we all know the taxman always prevails, as he did in this early case. So… at the time, our illustrious President Washington sent a force of militia to help along this mostly unknown scene in American history. This small insurrection was to go down in history as the 'Whiskey Rebellion.' Though these inevitable taxes soon became part of the business equation of Whiskey production, early settlers opposed to these taxes had little choice but to move farther and farther out of reach of the long arm of the tax collectors. So… going out into 'Indian Territory' was an early fact of life for these Whiskey loving forefathers. Many newly immigrated but disgruntled Irish, Scottish and Dutch farmer / distillers soon found themselves in southern Indiana and Kentucky where the water was pure and the corn grew tall.

Bourbon Whiskey

Bourbon originates from 'Bourbon County, Kentucky.' It is a liquor distilled from no less than 51% corn, balanced with barley, wheat and or rye, fermented with the clean crisp limestone spring waters of the region, filtered and distilled in pot stills 'in Kentucky.' Each house jealously guarding the sometimes 'generations old' family bourbon recipe, aged from at least two years, but more commonly four to 12 years in new white oak casks. These aging barrels are first charred inside to 'caramelize' the natural sugars out of the wood then the spirits are allowed on the wood for their maturation. This unique form of aging is revealed in the subtle, mellow and slightly sweet flavor to this fine elixir. Usually full bodied with a hint of smoke and caramel, Bourbon Whiskey has a proud 200 Year History. Concerning other counties or regions that this distinctive elixir comes from... Only 'Kentucky Whiskey' is considered 'real' 'Bourbon Whiskey'.

It is rumored that an old Baptist Minister named 'Elijah Craig' was the first to brew real Bourbon Whiskey. A tradition that lives on proudly today.

Tennessee Whiskey

A liquor distilled similarly to that of Bourbon Whiskey, though brewed next door in Tennessee. It is fermented with the clean crisp limestone spring waters of Tennessee, filtered, then distilled in pot stills 'in Tennessee,' each house jealously guarding the sometimes 'generations old' family whiskey recipe. Here just before the barreling stage, Tennessee Whiskey undergoes a unique 'Mellowing process.' This is what distinguishes 'Tennessee' from 'Bourbon.' The added filtration of Tennessee Whiskey is so significant, that 'by law' there is a separate category for 'Tennessee Whiskey.' This mellowing process is a slow filtering of the spirit over charcoal; the charcoal produced by burning seasoned sugar maple tree wood. Over a period of ten days the spirits are filtered through this charcoal and the end result is a unique 'Tennessee' smoky sweetness. It is then aged in oak casks. This unique form of filtration is revealed in the extremely smooth nature and a mellow, slightly sweet flavor, usually full bodied with a hint of smoke and caramel. Props to the House of Jack Daniels ® for their vision and proud heritage of this unique spirit. Their sour mash whiskey is a fine example of the distinctive Tennessee heritage.

Brandy

Brandy is an alcoholic liquor distilled in pot stills from fermented fruit juice or wine. Aged in oak barrels, and bottled according to age. This product is most renown originating from a region called 'Cognac,' France, although there are many brandies from many places. It is said that "All Cognac is Brandy Yet Not All Brandy is Cognac." This is to illustrate that the product exists outside of Cognac, France, but most notably, from this revered region. There is Armagnac a similar spirit and region in France, yet, to the master distillers, a 'distinctly' different product. Brandy is made all over the world. Cognac is made in France.
So.......Cognac is produced, grown, harvested, fermented, distilled, aged and bottled in the region of Cognac, France. Since the early 17th century this spirit has a decorated and proud heritage. These Cognacs are carefully scrutinized and graded by age.

'VS' = Very Special = aged 4 to 5 years.

'VSOP' = Very Superior Old Pale = aged 7 to 10 years.

'VO' = Very Old = aged 10 to 15 years.

'XO' = Extra Old = aged 20 to 50 years.

Brandy, like Rum and Tequila, is an agricultural spirit. Unlike grain spirits such as Whiskey, Vodka, and Gin, which are made throughout the year from grain that can be harvested and stored, Brandy is dependent on the seasons, the ripening of the base fruit, and the production of the wine from which it is made. Types of Brandies, originally at least, tended to be location-specific. Cognac, for example, is a town and region in France that gave its name to the local Brandy. French Brandy called Cognac.

The word Brandy comes from the Dutch word brandewijn, ("burnt wine"), which is how the straight-forward Dutch traders who introduced it to Northern Europe from Southern France and Spain in the 16th century described wine that had been 'burnt,' or boiled, in order to distill it. The origins of Brandy can be traced back to the expanding Moslem Mediterranean states in the 7th and 8th centuries. Arab alchemists experimented with distilling grapes and other fruits in order to make medicinal spirits. Brandy, in its broadest definition, is a spirit made from fruit juice or fruit pulp and fruit skins.

Liqueurs & Cordials

Liqueurs, Cordials, Schnapps, Anise, and Bitters are terms that cover a wide variety of types of spirits. What they all share in common is that they are all flavored spirits. Liqueurs, (also known as Cordials), are sweet, flavor-infused spirits that are categorized according to the flavoring agent like fruits, nuts, herbal and spice blends, creams and others. The word liqueur comes from the Latin liquifacere, (to dissolve), and refers to the dissolving of flavorings in the spirits. Artificial flavorings are strictly regulated in most countries, and where allowed, must be prominently labeled as such. Top-quality liqueurs are produced by distillation of either the fermented flavor materials or the spirit in which they have been infused. Many liqueurs use finished spirits such as Cognac, Rum or Whisky as their base. Others macerate fruit or other flavorings in a neutral spirit. Crèmes, (crème de menthe, crème de cacao, etc.), are liqueurs with a primary flavor a single, dominant flavor rather than a mix.

What is a cordial or liqueur?
According to the Webster's dictionary it is "a spirituous liquor flavored with various aromatic substances, usually sweetened, and often brandy-based. Liqueurs are usually made by steeping the flavoring material in the spirit." Knowing that they are often brandy-based, it is useful to know that brandy is distilled from wine. As identified, cordials and liqueurs are usually made by adding some flavor to alcohol, via an infusion.

All liqueurs are blends, even those with a primary flavor. A touch of vanilla is added to crème de cacao in order to emphasize the chocolate. Citrus flavor notes sharpen the presentation of anise. Herbal liqueurs may contain dozens of different flavor elements that a master blender manipulates to achieve the desired flavor profile.
Liqueurs are not usually aged for any great length of time, (although their base spirit may be), but may undergo resting stages during their production in order to allow the various flavors to "marry" into a harmonious blend.
Liqueurs can be hard to classify, but regardless of flavor they can be broadly divided into several categories.

Generics are liqueurs of a particular type (Crème de Cacao or Curaçao, for example) that can be made by any producer.

Proprietaries are liqueurs with trademarked names that are made according to a specific formula.

Schnapps is a general term used for an assortment of white and flavored spirits.

Anise-Flavored Spirits can vary widely in style depending on the country of origin. They can be dry or very sweet, low or high proof, distilled from fermented aniseed or macerated in neutral spirit.

Bitters are the modern-day descendants of medieval medical potions and are marketed as having at least some vaguely therapeutic value as stomach settlers or hangover cures. They tend to be flavored with herbs, roots, and botanicals, contain lower quantities of fruit and sugar than liqueurs, and have astringent notes in the palate.

Chapter 3
Welcome to
Napa Valley
Wine

The World of Wine

Wine has been made and enjoyed long before anything was being recorded, yet it seems that wine has had great importance to man for thousands of years. Many civilizations have left countless depictions of wine, wine enjoyment, cultivation, storage, transport to distant lands, and sometimes even tragedy; there are shipwrecks with wine that are 2500 years old. Wine recovered from the holds of these ancient merchant ships was stored in giant amphorae and topped with olive oil as their 'cork' then… dashed to the bottom of the sea for a couple of millennia…It is said that, "Though the ancient wine may have seen better times, it's at least drinkable." There are frescos and murals, chisels in stone, clay tablets, papyrus, hieroglyphics, jewelry and statuary. Even the ancient Greeks worshiped a God of Wine. His name is Bacchus. Throughout history and before, wine has been a powerful element of almost every civilization up until contemporary times. The elixir of choice is always determined by what organic stores are available to the local population. Grapes of many, many varieties have always been available to myriad peoples and lands.

The Old World

True organized modern day wine grape cultivation has its strong roots in Europe. Most notably, today, in France and Italy but must also be mentioned in Greece, Spain and Portugal and ancient Mesopotamia. These countries and regions make up the main areas of 'old world' wine production today. These wines are generally known as and sold by the region of the wine's origin. The kind of grape used is more important to the winemaker and less to the consumer. These wines are most often sold as 'Burgundy' for example, or 'Chianti,' rather than 'Pinot Noir' or 'Sangiovese.'

The New World The great wine vines of Old World Europe were brought to the new world, planted and cultivated here in North America, South America and more recently Australia and South Africa. These wines are generally known as and sold by the grape. The region where the grape is from and the kind of grape is more important to the winemaker <u>but</u> the wine is first categorized as the grape of origin... Chardonnay, Sauvignon Blanc, Pinot Noir, Zinfandel etc., then the region of origin is the next on the priority list of importance. There are many, many kinds of grapes, each having its distinct characteristics ultimately yielding flavors and textures.

Wine Making Process

Wine making has taken many forms over the years. Proud farmers and winemakers each tweaking 'their' process... grapes, rootstock, when to plant, when to harvest, blending, percentage recipes and techniques. All important decisions for great wine!

Crushing and de-stemming the grapes

The grapes just arriving in the cellar are crushed and de-stemmed to release their juice and pulp. This is called 'must.' The 'must' obtained is put in a tank to go trough the process of fermentation.

Alcoholic Fermentation is a natural process. Yeasts living on the grapes as well as an introduction of specially selected yeasts by the winemaker. The winemaker will also assist the action of the yeasts by maintaining the temperature around 25°C to 30°C and by ventilating the must regularly. Under 25°C the wine will not have enough body, above 30°C, the wine will be too tannic. The fermentation process goes on for four to 10 days until the initial fermentation and then, often a secondary fermentation called malolactic fermentation.

Malolactic Fermentation This a secondary fermentation, initiated by the winemaker. It is the process during which the malic acid of wine changes into lactic acid and carbonic gas under the action of bacteria living in the wine.

Maceration

This is the period when the tannic elements and the color of the skin diffuse in the fermented juice. The contact between the liquid (must) and the solid elements (skin, pits and sometimes stem) will give body, tannins, complexity and color to the wine. This stage, will often prove the talent of the winemaker. Wines destined to be kept long need a lot of tannin, so the maceration needs to be longer. The wine will macerate for several days, maybe several weeks.

Punch Down

While the wine is macerating, someone will take a long pole with a flat round end on it, and physically "punch down" the floating must solids.
Sometimes this process is done mechanically.

Raking

The wine is separated from the solids, the pomace. The wine obtained by raking is called "free run wine" or "vin de goutte." Sometimes the pomace is pressed in order to extract the juice it still contains. This wine is called "press wine" or "vin de presse." It is richer in tannin. Depending on the winemaker's taste or the local habit, free run wine and press wine are locally popular, but not marketed widely.

Stabilization

When fermentation is over, and the winemaker it satisfied, the wine is put in cask and raked, just like a red wine. The length of time “on oak” is determined by the winemaker. Only after sufficient time has elapsed will the wine be ready for bottling. Only after the winemaker says it’s ready, is it bottled.

During the “Oak” Winemakers often choose oak casks of different varieties to utilize the different complexities contained within each. This can add the right combination of flavors which maximizes the wine’s character.

Tannin is an essential element for aging. White wines have less tannins than red wines. This is why white wine does not keep as long as red wine.

The wine making process is finished but the wine is not. To be able to age and improve, the wine must be clarified again. Then the beverage will be put in oak casks where it will stabilize.

The control of the temperature is essential. It has to be maintained around 18° C. Which is why many wine storage vaults are “cellars” or “caves.” These natural or manmade, usually underground, areas maintain their own static and cool temperature so they are the perfect choice to age wine.

White wines present a large variety of tastes: creamy, tart, fruity, sweet, dry, slightly-dry, big, round, mellow, oaky, malo, sparkling, clean, flinty... White wine can be enjoyed on any occasion. Before, with or after a meal, red meat or curry; anything goes...

You don't have to match your colors any longer.

Just enjoy what makes you happy. Red wine also... If you like it, enjoy it! It doesn't matter that you're having fish or chicken.

Wine today is also keeping up with the times by earnestly pursuing the "green" way of doing business. The modern wine business and its executives are striving to make their operations as low impact as possible regarding the environment. They are also now actively growing and producing "organic" or "bio-dynamically" farmed grapes, and, importantly, marketing these wines as such.
This movement seems to be catching on with consumers and aficionados alike. Stay tuned for more advancements in the world of viticulture.

Sparkling Wine & Champagne

The Benedictine Monk Dom Perignon is reputed to have exclaimed, when drinking champagne, "It's like drinking the stars!" Champagne's magic comes as much from its bubbles as from its taste. In fact, it is sad that most people acquire their total knowledge of sparkling wines from what is offered at weddings. What is a Champagne? What is a sparkling wine? All wines which undergo a second fermentation, and are thus carbonated, are “sparkling wines.” This wine is bottled and corked quickly after fermentation. When the bubbles, (CO2 Gas), are still in the wine. This way those bubbles escape only after you’ve cracked open a fresh bottle of bubbly. Sounds kinda nice doesn’t it? All wine produced in this manner is called “Sparkling Wine,” but only sparkling wines grown, made and bottled in Champagne, France, are properly called Champagne. One can seldom go wrong with any true Champagne. But there is great variety in the rest of the world’s sparkling wines. **Champagne** has launched thousands of ships, entangled billions of lovers, toasted millions of weddings and special occasions, attended countless parties, and shared untold special moments between people.

Champagne also benefited when the cathedral at Reims was chosen in 987 AD, as the coronation site for the French King Hugh Capet, establishing Reims as the spiritual capital of medieval France. In fact, 37 kings of France were crowned there between 816 and 1825. The monasteries in Champagne with the economic assistance of the crown, were to make wine production a serious venture until the French Revolution in 1789. Before the mid-1600's there was no Champagne as we think of it. For centuries the wines were all *still* wines and were held in high re-gard by the nobility of Europe. The cool climate of the region and its effect on the wine making process was to play an important part in changing all of that. For Dom Pérignon and his contemporaries, sparkling wine was not the desired end product. It was a sign of poor wine making. He spent a great deal of time trying to prevent the bubbles and the unstableness of this "mad wine." He was not able to prevent the bubbles, but he did develop the art of blending. He not only blended different grapes, but the juice from the same grape grown in different vineyards. Dom Pérignon died in 1715, but in his 47 years as the cellar master at the Abby of Hautvillers, he laid down the basic principles still used in making Champagne and still wines today.

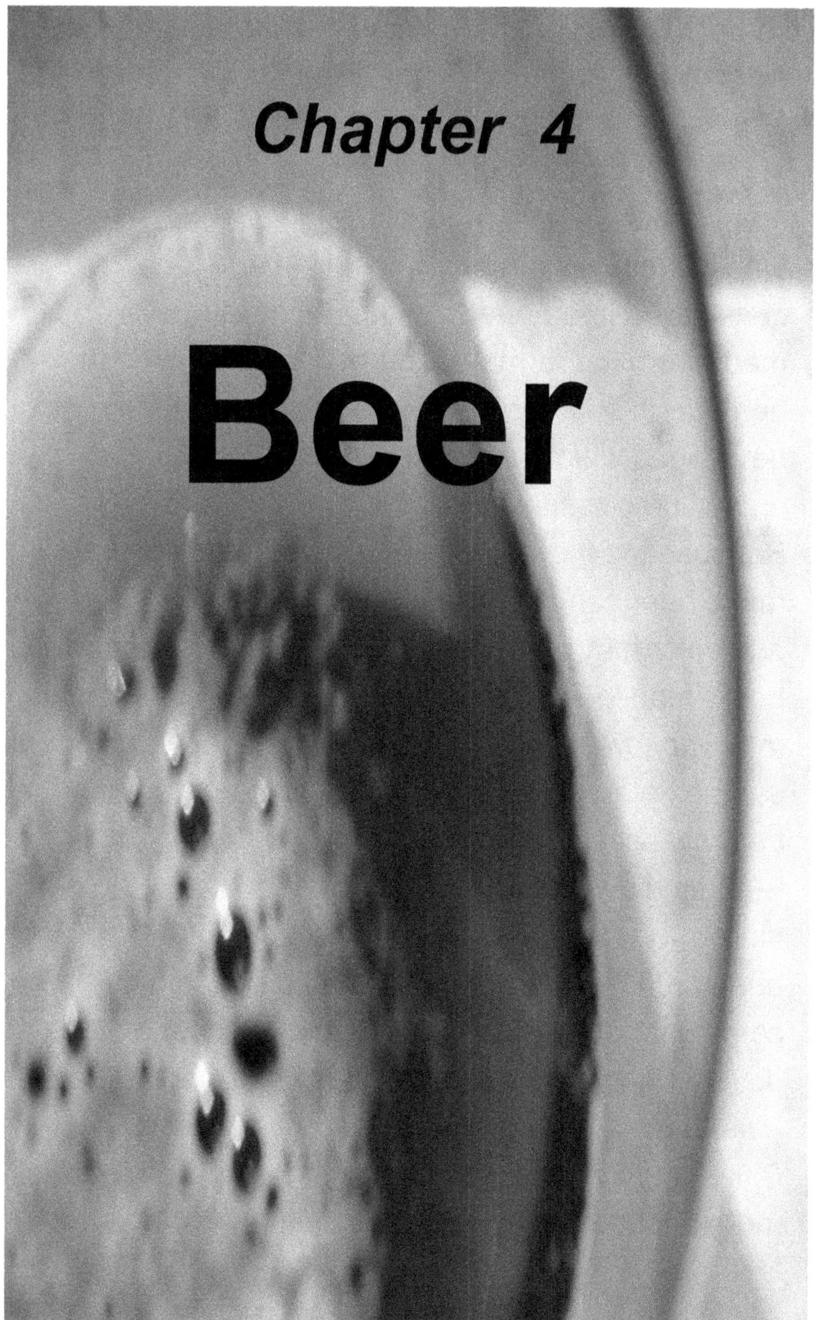
Chapter 4
Beer

Beer is the world's oldest and most popular alcoholic beverage. It is produced through the fermentation of starch-based material, fermentation of yeast and cereal grains, hops, barley and many, many other organic products.

Only beverages produced by this method are considered to be beer. Neither alcoholic beverages made from the fermentation of sugars derived from non-starch sources, (e.g., grape juice or honey), *nor* beverages which are distilled after fermentation should be classified as such.

Because the ingredients and procedures used to make beer can differ, characteristics such as taste and color may also vary. While local names for beers made with the same methods and ingredients may vary, the similarities of method and ingredients can be detected to form a study of the nature of beer styles.

But I am remiss... Why don't we start at the beginning? OK... So... Somewhere around 3000 BC or about 5000 years ago, sustainable society was coming together slowly yet surely... because of the advent of agriculture, which was necessary to be able to feed large groups of people consistently. Cities and city states began to emerge and required more and more organized agriculture.

Perhaps simultaneously in Mesopotamia, (present day Middle East), and Mesoamerica, (present day South America), religious consumption became of great value to these ancient civilizations. Ceremonial use of these elixirs was very popular throughout history and before... Recreational use to these fine varied brews was, and is still enjoyed by many across the globe. It has taken root and is now woven into the fabric of our society. No matter... every society or grouping of people, utilized what was available to them. Of course one of the most popular and cost effective of these products was grain. There are many forms of grains, some of these grains, were hard and bitter. Picture the woman of the house, preparing the daily meals, or more likely the family ration of grain. These would be prepared in as much variety as possible. She wants to make her family happy. So one day... this fine woman... whether she be from Persia or Argentina ... makes a mash of grain on her grinding stone. To this mash, she adds water... maybe heated over her fire. She mixes some herbs & spices. The lady of the house has prepared a fine meal of mush for her family. Some of this she serves to her family... but some she saves.

This is stored somewhere... Probably with a layer of water on top. Well somewhere nearby... traveling on the winds, are some naturally occurring "yeasts." Like the white frosting that you may see on a wine grape cluster; that is yeast. So this yeast finds its way to the ground mash of grains and water. Well... now we have all the components of making beer. Grains, heat, water and yeast. So the leftovers soon came to be noticed as having a different effect on the body and mind. A somewhat puzzling one, yet pleasurable... So... Our fine maiden, making dinner for her family... may have accidentally become the first brew master. People from miles around were talking about her magic meal. The food that makes you feel good. Well as time progressed... these foods became drinks, and fast became an overwhelming force in many, many cultures. Religious consumption was of great value to many ancient civilizations.

Chapter 5
Cocktail
Recipes

ALABAMA SLAMMER

Ingredients	Amounts	Preparation
Highball Glass	12 oz	Serving glass
Amaretto	1/2 oz.	Pour all ingredients
Peach Flavored Whiskey	1/2 oz.	Into a highball serving glass filled with ice
Sloe Gin	1/2 oz.	In the order listed here
Orange Juice	4 oz.	Fresh OJ is best
Orange Wedge	1 each	Finish with an orange

AMARETTO SOUR

Ingredients	Amounts	Preparation
Bucket Glass	12 oz	Serving glass
Amaretto	1 1/2oz.	Build the Amaretto and sweet & sour into a mixing glass
Sweet & Sour	2 oz.	Full of ice, squeeze your fruit wedges
Lemon Squeeze	1 each	Shake & pour into your serving glass
Lime Squeeze	1 each	
Orange Cherry	1 each 1 each	Garnish with an orange and a cherry

APPLE MARTINI

Ingredients	Amounts	Preparation
Martini Glass	6 - 10 oz	Serving glass *Pre-chilled*
Vodka	1 oz.	Build into mixing glass filled with ice
Apple Schnapps	1 oz.	Pour all the ingredients
Lemon Lime Soda	3 oz.	Shake and strain into a martini glass
Sweet & Sour	*2 oz.	*Optional, replaces lemon lime soda
Cherry	1 each	*or use a red apple slice

BAY BREEZE

Ingredients	Amounts	Preparation
Highball Glass	12 oz.	Serving glass
Vodka	1 1/2 oz.	Fill highball glass with ice
Pineapple Juice	4 oz.	Build vodka & pineapple into glass
Cranberry Juice	1/2 oz.	Gently pour in cranberry
		Do not mix up! This drink should appear two tone
Lemon Wedge	1 each	On the edge of the glass

B 52

Ingredients	Amounts	Preparation
Shot Glass	2 - 3 oz.	Serving glass
Coffee Liqueur	3/4 oz.	In a shot glass
Irish Cream Liqueur	3/4 oz.	Carefully & slowly 'layer' these ingredients Use a spoon or a cherry
Orange Liqueur	1/2 oz.	It should finish as a three layer shot. *Be sure to pour liqueurs in order!

BLACK MARTINI

Ingredients	Amounts	Preparation
Martini Glass	6 - 10 oz.	Serving glass *Pre-chilled*
Vodka	2 oz.	Pour vodka over the ice in a mixing glass
		Shake & strain into a martini glass
Raspberry Liqueur	1 oz.	Pour liqueur in 'slowly' down the side of the glass
		Create two layers
Lemon Twist		Garnish with a twist

BLACK RUSSIAN

Ingredients	Amounts	Preparation
Rocks Glass	8 - 10 oz.	Serving glass
Vodka	1 1/2 oz.	Fill rocks glass with ice
Coffee Liqueur	1 1/2 oz.	Build drink over ice into serving glass No garnish

BLUE CHEESE MARTINI

Ingredients	Amounts	Preparation
Martini Glass	6 - 10 oz.	Serving glass *Pre-chilled*
Vodka	3 oz.	Fill a mixing glass with ice
Blue Cheese	a little	Pour vodka over the ice
Green Olives	3 or 4	Shake 'vigorously' and strain into a martini glass
"You'll want more olives after you taste them"		Garnish with prepared blue cheese stuffed green olives

BLOODY MARY

Ingredients	Amounts	Preparation
Highball Glass	10 - 12 oz.	Serving glass
Vodka	1 1/2 oz.	Fill salt rimmed serving glass with ice
Tomato Juice	4 oz.	Add vodka & tomato juice
Horseradish	1/4 tsp.	Then add all the spicy stuff on top
Worcestershire Sauce Hot Sauce	2 dashes 4 dashes	It's best to let your guest mix it up
Spices; Salt, Pepper, Celery Salt, & Lime Juice	to taste go for it!	Garnish with celery, shrimp, lime & olive
Olives and Lime	Shrimp & Celery	Celery is the most common garnish

BLUE HAWAIIAN

Ingredients	Amounts	Preparation
Highball Glass	12 oz.	Serving glass
Light Rum	1/2 oz.	Fill your serving glass with ice
Blue Curacao Orange Juice	1/2 oz. 1 oz.	Pour light rum, juices & blue curacao over the ice
Dark Rum	1/2 oz.	Float dark rum on top of drink
Pineapple Juice	1 oz.	
Sweet & Sour	1 oz.	
Orange & Cherry	1 each	Place garnish onto the rim of the glass

BRANDY ALEXANDER

Ingredients	Amounts	Preparation
Martini Glass	6 - 10 oz.	Serving glass *Pre-chilled*
Brandy	1 oz.	Pour all ingredients into a mixing glass full of ice, then into a blender
Crème de Cocoa	1/2 oz.	Blend until thick and smooth
Half & Half	2 oz.	Serve in a martini glass
Nutmeg		Garnish with a sprinkle of nutmeg

BUTTERY NIPPLE

Ingredients	Amounts	Preparation
Shot Glass	2 - 3 oz.	Serving glass
Butterscotch	1 oz.	In a shot glass
Irish Cream Liqueur	1 oz.	Carefully and slowly
		Layer these ingredients
		It should finish as a two layer cocktail

CADILLAC MARGARITA

Ingredients	Amounts	Preparation
Margarita Glass	12 oz.	Serving glass
Tequila	1 oz.	Pour tequila, triple sec, sweet & sour, lime juice & limes
Triple Sec	1/2 oz.	Over ice in a mixing glass
Sweet & Sour Fresh Lime Juice	1 1/2 oz. 1 splash	Shake until 'frothy' and pour into a salt rimmed margarita glass
Lime Wedges	3 squeezes	Finish with a generous splash of orange liqueur on top
Orange Liqueur	1/2 oz.	This is the 'Golden Cadillac' part
'Fresh' O J* Salt Rim	1 oz. kosher salt	*Optional &highly recommended

CAPE CODDER

Ingredients	Amounts	Preparation
Highball Glass	12 oz.	Serving glass
Vodka	1 1/2 oz.	Fill highball with ice
Cranberry Juice	3 1/2 oz.	Build your drink into the glass, always pour the alcohol first
Lime Wedge	1 each	Finish with a lime wedge on the rim of the glass

COSMOPOLITAN

Ingredients	Amounts	Preparation
Martini Glass	6 - 10 oz.	Serving glass *Pre-chilled*
Vodka	1 1/2 oz.	Pour all ingredi- ents into a mixing glass full of ice
Triple Sec	1 oz.	*Traditional recipe calls for a 'citrus' vodka
Cranberry Juice	2 oz.	Use a real squeeze of lemon to get a little pulp
Squeeze of Lemon	1 each	Shake & strain into a martini glass
Lemon Twist	1 each	Finish with a lemon twist

CHAMPAGNE COCKTAIL

Ingredients	Amounts	Preparation
Champagne Flute	6 - 8 oz.	Serving glass
Sugar Cube	1 each	Shake bitters onto a sugar cube, saturate it
Bitters	3 dashes	Fill a champagne glass with champagne
Champagne	5 1/2 oz.	Drop the saturated sugar cube in 'gently'
Lemon Twist	*It needs the time release of the cube	*Don't try it with a 'packet of sugar' It won't work
Lemon Twist		Finish with a twist of lemon

CHOCOLATE MARTINI

Ingredients	Amounts	Preparation
Martini Glass	6 - 10 oz.	Serving glass *Pre-chilled*
Vodka	2 oz.	Pour vodka & crème de cocoa into a mixing glass full of ice
'White' or Clear Crème de Cocoa	1 oz.	Shake vigorously Let 'cure' for 10 seconds.
Chocolate Swirl	1 swirl	Strain into a martini glass with a swirl of chocolate
Cherry		Garnish with a cherry

COLORADO BULLDOG

Ingredients	Amounts	Preparation
Rocks Glass	6 - 8 oz.	Serving glass
Vodka	1 oz.	Build all ingredients
Coffee Liqueur	1 oz.	Into a rocks glass
Half & Half	1 oz.	Full of ice
Cola	1 oz.	No garnish Tasty cocktail!

CUBA LIBRE

Ingredients	Amounts	Preparation
Bucket Glass	10 - 12 oz.	Serving glass
Light or Spiced Rum	1 1/2 oz.	Build all ingredients
Cola	3 1/2 oz.	Into a bucket glass
Lime	1 each	Full of ice
*This drink is different from a rum & cola because it gets a lime		Lime garnish

DAIQUIRI

Ingredients	Amounts	Preparation
Wine Goblet	14 - 20 oz.	Serving glass
Light Rum	1 1/2 oz.	Build all ingredients, except the wedge of lime, into a mixing glass full of ice
Sweet & Sour Lime Squeeze	3 oz. 3 each	Then pour all ingredients into a blender and squeeze the limes. blend until smooth
Orange Wedge	1 each	Don't blend the rind of the limes
Cherry	1 each	Serve in a wine glass

DAIQUIRI / STRAWBERRY

Ingredients	Amounts	Preparation
Wine Goblet	14 - 20 oz.	Serving Glass
Light Rum Sweet & Sour	1 1/2 oz. 1 oz.	Pour all ingredients, except the wedge of lime, into a mixing glass full of ice
Strawberry Strawberry Puree	1 each 2 oz.	Then pour all ingredients into a blender & squeeze the limes, blend until smooth
Lime Squeeze	3 each	Don't blend the rind of the lime
Strawberry	1 each	Serve in a wine glass

ELECTRIC ICED TEA

Ingredients	Amounts	Preparation
Highball Glass	12 oz.	Serving Glass
Vodka	1/2 oz.	Build all ingredients
Gin	1/2 oz.	Into the highball serving glass
Light Rum	1/2 oz.	Full of ice
Triple Sec	1/2 oz.	
Lemon Lime Soda	1 oz.	In this order
Sweet & Sour	2 oz.	
Blue Curacao	1/4 oz.	Add just a <u>small</u> splash, last
Orange Wedge Cherry	1 each	Garnish with both

FRENCH CONNECTION

Ingredients	Amounts	Preparation
Snifter Glass	10 - 20 oz.	Serving glass
Brandy	1 oz.	Combine both ingredients
Grand Marnier®	1 oz.	Directly into the snifter glass
	No garnish	*Pre-Heating the glass is optional & recommended
		*Just fill the snifter with very hot water for about one minute, when the glass is warm dispense the good stuff

FRENCH MARTINI

Ingredients	Amounts	Preparation
Martini Glass	6 - 10 oz.	Serving glass *Pre-chilled*
Vodka	2 oz.	Pour Vodka and pineapple juice over the ice in a mixing glass
Pineapple Juice	2 oz.	Shake and strain into a martini glass
Raspberry Liqueur	1 oz.	Then pour liqueur in 'slowly' down the inside of the glass
Lemon Twist	1 each	Try to finish with two layers. Gar-nish with a twist

FRENCH 75

Ingredients	Amounts	Preparation
Martini Glass	6 - 10 oz.	Serving glass *Pre-chilled*
Gin	3 oz.	Pour Gin over the ice in a mixing glass, then squeeze the lemon juice
Lemon Juice	1/2 lemon	Shake & strain into a martini glass
Champagne	1 oz.	Pour Champagne in last
Lemon Twist	1 each	Garnish with a twist

FUZZY NAVEL

Ingredients	Amounts	Preparation
Highball Glass	10 - 12 oz.	Serving glass
Vodka	1 1/2 oz.	Build all ingredients into the highball serving glass full of ice
Peach Schnapps	1/2 oz.	
Orange Juice	2 oz.	
Orange Wedge	1 each	Garnish with a wedge of orange

GREYHOUND

Ingredients	Amounts	Preparation
Bucket Glass	12 oz.	Serving glass
Vodka	1 1/2 oz.	Build the ingredients
Grapefruit Juice	4 oz.	Directly into the highball serving glass filled with ice
Lime Wedge	1 each	Garnish with a lime wedge

GIBSON

Ingredients	Amounts	Preparation
Martini Glass	6 - 10 oz.	Serving glass *Pre-chilled*
Gin or Vodka	3 1/2 oz.	Pour gin or vodka & vermouth into a mixing glass full of ice
'Dry' Vermouth	1/4 oz. or less	Shake vigorously Let 'cure' for 10 seconds
Baby Bar Onions	3 each	Strain into a martini glass

GIMLET

Ingredients	Amounts	Preparation
Rocks Glass	6 - 8 oz.	Serving glass
Vodka or Gin	1 1/2 oz.	Build the ingredients directly into the rocks serving glass filled with ice
Lime Juice Concentrate	1 splash	Pour alcohol first, then lime, squeeze the lime wedges
Fresh Lime Juice	4 lime wedges	Pulp is ok, this drink is tart
Lime Wedge	1 each	Garnish with a lime wedge

GODFATHER

Ingredients	Amounts	Preparation
Rocks Glass	6 - 8 oz.	Serving glass
Scotch	1 1/2 oz.	Build all ingredients
Amaretto	1 1/2 oz.	Directly into the rocks serving glass filled with ice
		No garnish

GRASSHOPPER

Ingredients	Amounts	Preparation
Martini Glass	6 - 10 oz.	Serving glass *Pre-chilled*
Vodka	1 oz.	Pour all ingredi-ents into a mixing glass full of ice
White Crème de Cocoa	1/4 oz.	Shake vigorously until smooth
White Crème de Menthe	1/2 oz.	A little frothy is good
Green Crème de Menthe	1/4 oz.	Strain cocktail into serving glass
Half & Half	2 oz.	Sprinkle with nutmeg
Chocolate	a Little	How about a little chocolate swirl
Nutmeg	a sprinkle	Finish with a cherry

HARVEY WALLBANGER

Ingredients	Amounts	Preparation
Highball Glass	12 oz.	Serving glass
Vodka	1 oz.	Build the vodka & OJ directly into the highball serving glass full of ice
Orange Juice	4 oz.	Float the Galliano® on top of the cocktail by pouring it in last
Galliano®	1/2 oz.	
Orange Wedge	1 each	Garnish with an orange wedge

Ingredients	Amounts	Preparation
Champagne Flute	6 - 8 oz.	Serving glass
Champagne or Sparkling Wine	5 oz.	Fill the flute with champagne, leave room for a little juice
Guava Juice	1 oz.	Slowly pour the guava nectar into the champagne
Cherry	1 each	Garnish with a cherry

HOT BUTTERED RUM

Ingredients	Amounts	Preparation
Coffee Glass	6 - 8 oz.	*Pre-heating the glass is essential
Dark or Spiced Rum Hot Water	1 1/2 oz. 4 oz.	fill the glass with very hot water, when the glass is hot discard the water
Brown Sugar	2 tsp.	Begin with the butter & brown sugar at the bottom of glass
Butter Nutmeg	1 tsp. A sprinkle	Pour the rum in next, then fresh hot water
Cinnamon	and a stick	Sprinkle with nutmeg & cinnamon & serve

HOT TODDY

Ingredients	Amounts	Preparation
Coffee Glass	6 - 8 oz.	*Pre-heating the glass is essential
Bourbon Hot Water	1 1/2 oz. 4 oz.	Fill the glass with hot water, when the glass is hot, discard the water
Orange Liqueur	1 oz.	Dip the rim in sugar. Nice!
Granulated Sugar	2 tsp.	Then 2 tsp. sugar at the bottom of your heated glass
Cinnamon and Nutmeg	A sprinkle and a stick	Next goes in the bourbon then fresh hot water
		Serve with a stick of cinnamon

HURRICANE

Ingredients	Amounts	Preparation
Hurricane Glass	14 - 22 oz	Serving glass
Light Rum	1 oz.	Build all of the ingredients into a mixing glass full of ice
Passion Fruit Juice	5 oz.	Shake & pour into serving glass
Lime Juice	1/2 lime	Squeeze it fresh
Dark Rum* *Optional	1 oz.	Dark rum goes on top as a floater
Lemon	1 each	Garnish with a wedge of lemon

IRISH COFFEE

Ingredients	Amounts	Preparation
Coffee Glass	6 - 8 oz.	Serving glass *Pre-heated*
Irish Whiskey	1 1/2 oz.	Pre-heat the coffee glass
Irish Cream Liqueur	1/2 oz.	Then a sugar rim & add all your ingredients
Coffee	3 oz.	Then, pour the coffee. Leave some room for the whipped cream
Whipped Cream		Last is the whipped cream Pile it High!

KAMIKAZE

Ingredients	Amounts	Preparation
Rocks Glass	6 - 8 oz.	Serving glass
Vodka	2 oz.	Build the drink directly into the serving glass
Triple Sec	1 oz.	Begin with the vodka & triple sec
Lime Juice	1/4 oz.	Then the lime juice
Fresh Lime Wedges	3 each	Thoroughly squeeze three wedges of lime into the cocktail
Garnish with a lime wedge		You want some pulp in there!

KEOKE COFFEE

Ingredients	Amounts	Preparation
Coffee Glass	6 - 8 oz.	Serving glass *Pre-heated*
Brandy	3/4 oz.	Pre-heat the coffee glass
Coffee Liqueur	3/4 oz.	Then a sugar rim
Hot Coffee	3 oz	Then the brandy & coffee liqueur
Whipped Cream		Then pour the coffee. Leave some room for the whipped cream

KEY LIME MARTINI

Ingredients	Amounts	Preparation
Martini Glass	6 - 10 oz.	Serving glass *Pre-chilled*
Vanilla Vodka	1 1/2 oz.	Pour the vanilla vodka
Vanilla Schnapps Lime Juice	1/2 oz. 2 oz.	And all the rest of the ingredients.
Half & Half Pineapple Juice	1/2 oz. 1 oz.	'Rim' your glass with graham cracker crumbs
Lime Wedge	3 each	Squeeze thoroughly!
Graham Cracker Crumbs	enough to rim the glass	Shake & strain mixture into prepared, chilled, rimmed martini glass

KIR

Ingredients	Amounts	Preparation
Ingredients	Amounts	Preparation
Red Wine Goblet	14 - 20 oz.	Serving glass
Dry White Wine	6 oz.	Pour the white wine into a wine goblet
Crème de Cassis	3/4 oz.	Pour your choice of liqueur slowly down the side of the wine glass
* <u>or</u> Raspberry Liqueur	3/4 oz.	A pour spout works best
		You want to finish with a two layer cocktail

KIR ROYALE

Ingredients	Amounts	Preparation
Champagne Flute	6 - 8 oz.	Serving glass
Champagne or Sparkling Wine	5 oz.	Pour the sparkling wine or Champagne into a champagne flute
Crème de Cassis *	3/4 oz.	Pour the liqueur slowly down the side of the wine glass
* or Raspberry Liqueur	3/4 oz.	A pour spout works best
Lemon Twist	finish with a twist	You want to finish with a two layer cocktail

LEMON DROP MARTINI

Ingredients	Amounts	Preparation
Martini Glass	6 - 10 oz.	Serving glass *Pre-chilled*
Lemon or Citron Vodka Triple Sec	1 1/4 oz. 3/4 oz	Muddle thoroughly 3 lemon wedges and 1 tsp. of granulated sugar
Lemonade	2 oz.	Then... fill the mixing glass with ice & ingredients
Lemon Wedges	3 each	Vodka, triple sec, & lemonade
Granulated Sugar	rim the glass	Shake and strain into your chilled, sugar rimmed martini glass
Lemon Wedge	1 each	Garnish with a lemon wedge

LONG BEACH ICED TEA

Ingredients	Amounts	Preparation
Highball Glass	12 oz.	Serving glass
Vodka	1/2 oz.	Build all ingredients
Gin	1/2 oz.	Into the highball serving glass
Light Rum	1/2 oz.	Full of ice
Triple Sec	1/2 oz.	
Sweet & Sour	1/2 oz.	
Cranberry Juice	1 oz.	Add this last
Lemon Wedge	1 each	Garnish with a lemon wedge

LONG ISLAND ICED TEA

Ingredients	Amounts	Preparation
Highball Glass	12 oz.	Serving glass
Vodka	1/2 oz.	Build all ingredients
Gin	1/2 oz.	Into the highball serving glass
Light Rum	1/2 oz.	Full of ice
Triple Sec	1/2 oz.	
Sweet & Sour	1/2 oz.	
Cola	1 oz.	As dark as iced tea! Add this last
Lemon Wedge	1 each	Garnish with a lemon wedge

Ingredients	Amounts	Preparation
Highball Glass	12 oz.	Serving glass
Vodka	1 1/2 oz.	Build the ingredients directly into the highball serving glass full of ice
Orange Juice	3 1/2 oz	In the order listed
Cranberry Juice	1 splash	Pour cranberry in slowly
Orange Wedge	1 each	Don't mix it up
Cherry	1 each	Garnish with a nice wedge of fresh orange & a cherry

MAI TAI

Ingredients	Amounts	Preparation
Highball Glass	12 oz.	Serving glass
Light Rum	1 oz.	Build directly into the serving glass full of ice
Orange Juice	1 1/2 oz.	In the order listed, one at a time
Pineapple Juice	1 1/2 oz.	The juices will mix
Crème de Almond	1/4 oz.	This one will sink!
Dark Rum	1/2 oz.	This one will float!
Cocktail Umbrella	1 each	It should be a 3 layer cocktail
Orange & Cherry	1 each	Garnish with one each

MANHATTAN

Ingredients	Amounts	Preparation
Martini Glass	6 - 10 oz.	Serving glass *Pre-chilled*
Rye Whiskey	2 oz.	Pour whiskey, sweet vermouth & bitters into a mixing glass full of ice
Sweet Vermouth	1 oz. or less	Stir Slowly, or 'roll' cocktail between shaker & tin
Bitters	three shakes	Strain into a martini glass
Cherry	1 each	Garnish with a cherry

MARGARITA

Ingredients	Amounts	Preparation
Margarita Glass	12 oz.	Serving glass
Tequila Triple Sec	1 oz. 1/2 oz.	Add all ingredients into a mixing glass full of ice
Sweet & Sour	1 1/2 oz.	Shake until 'frothy'
Fresh Lime Juice Lime Wedges	Splash 3 squeezes	Pour all into your 'salt rimmed' margarita serving glass
'Fresh' O J	small splash	*Optional & highly recommended!
Salt Rim	kosher salt	Finish with a straw and a lime wedge

MARGARITA / CADILLAC

Ingredients	Amounts	Preparation
Margarita Glass	12 oz.	Serving glass
Tequila Triple Sec	1 oz. 1/2 oz.	Add all ingredients into a mixing glass full of ice
Sweet & Sour	1 1/2 oz.	Shake until 'frothy'
Fresh Lime Juice Lime Wedges	Splash 3 squeezes	Pour all into your 'salt rimmed' margarita serving glass
Orange Liqueur	1/2 oz.	Float on Top
Salt Rim	kosher salt	Finish with a straw and a lime

MARTINI / GIN

Ingredients	Amounts	Preparation
Martini Glass	6 - 10 oz.	Serving glass *Pre-chilled*
Gin	3 oz.	Pour gin & vermouth into a mixing glass full of ice
'Dry' Vermouth	6 drops	Stir Slowly, or 'roll' cocktail between
Green Olives	3 each	Strain into a martini glass
Some people like to 'stir' their gin martinis	This is quite acceptable	Garnish with olives, or a twist

MARTINI / VODKA

Ingredients	Amounts	Preparation
Martini Glass	6 - 10 oz.	Serving glass *Pre-chilled*
Vodka	3 oz.	Pour vodka & vermouth into a mixing glass full of ice
'Dry' Vermouth	6 drops	Shake vigorously
*Stirring is Optional		Let 'cure' for 10 seconds
Green Olives	3 each	Strain into a martini glass
		Garnish with olives, or a twist

MELON BALL

Ingredients	Amounts	Preparation
Highball Glass	12 oz.	Serving glass
Vodka	1 oz.	Build directly into the highball serving glass full of ice
Melon Liqueur	1/2 oz.	In the order listed here
Sweet & Sour	3 oz.	It will appear layered
Soda Water	1 oz.	Float soda on top
Lemon Wedge	1 each	This is a very pretty cocktail
Cherry	1 each	and tasty

MIMOSA

Ingredients	Amounts	Preparation
Champagne Flute	6 - 8 oz.	Serving glass
Champagne or Sparkling Wine	5 oz.	Fill the flute with the Champagne
Orange Juice	1 oz.	Slowly pour the orange juice into the Champagne
Orange Wedge	1 each	Garnish with an orange wedge

MIND ERASER

Ingredients	Amounts	Preparation
Bucket Glass	10 - 12 oz.	Serving glass
Vodka	2 oz.	Build directly into the serving glass full of ice
Coffee Liqueur	1 oz.	Vodka first, next the coffee liqueur
Half & Half	1 oz.	Then the half & half
Soda Water	2 oz.	Finally the soda water Pour gently, to create a 'layer' effect
Two Straws	two	Serve with two straws, to be enjoyed like a shot for two

MINT JULEP

Ingredients	Amounts	Preparation
Traditional Silver Cup or Rocks Glass	6 oz. 8-10 oz.	Serving cup Serving glass
Fresh Mint	Several leaves	'Muddle' the fresh mint & sugar into the bottom of the serving glass or the traditional silver cup
Powdered Sugar	1 tsp.	Then fill with crushed ice
Bourbon Whiskey	2 oz.	Next pour in the bourbon
Crushed Ice	Over flow with ice	Garnish with some fresh mint

MOJITO

Ingredients	Amounts	Preparation
Highball Glass	12 oz.	Serving glass
Mint Leaves	6 leaves	Begin with a mixing glass
Lime Wedges Light Rum	3 each 1 1/2 oz.	Muddle the lime wedges, mint leaves
Simple Syrup (Liquid Sugar)	1 oz.	Fill 2/3 mixing glass of ice. Add rum & lemonade
		Shake & pour into prepared sugar rimmed glass
Soda Water	2 oz.	Top this with soda water

MUD SLIDE

Ingredients	Amounts	Preparation
Rocks Glass	6 - 8 oz.	Serving glass
Vodka	1 oz.	Build into a rocks serving glass
Coffee Liqueur	1 oz.	Full of ice
Irish Cream Liqueur	1 oz.	* or layer the ingredients into a shot glass

NAVY GROG

Ingredients	Amounts	Preparation
Bucket Glass	10 - 12 oz.	Serving glass
Light Rum	1 oz.	Build directly into the serving glass full of ice
Orange Juice	1 oz.	In the order listed
Orange Curacao	1/2 oz.	The juices will mix
Orgeat Syrup	1/2 oz.	(Almond Syrup)
Dark Rum	1/2 oz.	This one will float!
Orange and Cherry	1 each	Garnish with an orange and a cherry

NEGRONI

Ingredients	Amounts	Preparation
Martini Glass	6 - 10 oz.	Serving glass *Pre-chilled*
Gin	1 oz.	Pour gin, Campari® and sweet vermouth into a mixing glass full of ice
Sweet Vermouth	1 oz.	'Shake vigorously'
Campari®	1 oz.	Let 'cure' for 10 seconds
		Strain into a martini glass
Twist	1 each	Garnish with a twist

NUTTY IRISHMAN

Ingredients	Amounts	Preparation
Coffee Glass	6 - 8 oz.	Serving glass *Pre-heated*
Irish Whiskey	1 oz.	Begin with a sugar rimmed 'hot' coffee glass
Irish Cream Liqueur	1/4 oz.	Then add the whiskey and liqueurs
Hazelnut Liqueur Hot Coffee	1/4 oz. 4 oz.	Pour the coffee, leave some room for the whipped cream
Fresh Whipped Cream		OK, now the whipped cream
Cinnamon Stick		

OATMEAL COOKIE

Ingredients	Amounts	Preparation
Shot Glass	2 - 3 oz.	Serving glass
Butterscotch Liqueur	1/2 oz.	Pour ingredients in the order listed
Peppermint Schnapps	1/2 oz.	Directly into the shot glass
Irish Cream Liqueur	1/2 oz.	This should be a clean three layer shot
		Use a spoon or cherry for pouring

OLD FASHIONED

Ingredients	Amounts	Preparation
Rocks Glass	6 - 8 oz.	Serving glass
Canadian Whiskey Granulated Sugar	3 oz. 1 Packet	Muddle the orange, the cherry, the packet of sugar and three dashes of bitters
Orange Wedge	1 each	Then, fill the glass with ice and pour in the whiskey
Cherry	1 each	Splash of soda or lemon lime soda at the end
Bitters	3 dashes	The garnish <u>is</u> the cherry and the orange wedge
Soda or Lemon Lime Soda	1 good splash	That you muddled

ORGASM

Ingredients	Amounts	Preparation
Rocks Glass *or Shot Glass	6 - 8 oz.	Serving glass
Amaretto	1/2 oz.	Pour ingredients in the order listed
Irish Cream Liqueur	1/2 oz.	Directly into the shot glass
Coffee Liqueur	1/2 oz.	Use a spoon or cherry for pouring
*also try on the rocks		

SCREAMING ORGASM

Ingredients	Amounts	Preparation
Rocks Glass *or Shot Glass	6 - 8 oz.	Serving glass
Vodka	1/2 oz.	Pour in ingredients in the order listed
Amaretto Irish Cream Liqueur	1/3 oz. 1/3 oz.	Directly into the shot glass or over the rocks in a rocks glass
Coffee Liqueur	1/3 oz.	Use a spoon or cherry for pouring
*or on the Rocks *This drink is the same as the Orgasm	Except that you add vodka	

PINA COLADA

Ingredients	Amounts	Preparation
Wine Goblet	14 - 20 oz.	Serving glass
Light Rum Orange Juice	1 1/2 oz. 1/2 oz.	Pour all ingredients into a mixing glass full of ice
Pineapple Juice Coconut Syrup Lime Squeeze	1 1/2 oz. 1 oz. 2 Each	Then pour all ingredients into a blender & squeeze the limes blend until smooth
Half & Half	1 splash	Serve in a wine glass
Orange and a Cherry	1 each	Orange & cherry garnish

PLANTERS PUNCH

Ingredients	Amounts	Preparation
Highball Glass	14 - 20 oz	Serving glass
Light Rum Lemon Wedge Lime Wedge	1 oz. 2 each 2 each	Pour light rum & juices into a highball glass full of ice
Orange Juice	1 1/2 oz.	Float the dark rum at the end
Pineapple Juice Grenadine	1 1/2 oz. 1 splash	Grenadine & dark rum are poured in last
Dark Rum	1/2 oz.	Grenadine will sink & the rum will float
Orange & Cherry	1 each	Serve with an orange & a cherry

PURPLE HOOTER

Ingredients	Amounts	Preparation
Martini Glass	6 - 10 oz.	Serving glass *Pre-chilled*
Vodka	1 1/2 oz.	Pour the vodka & pineapple juice into a mixing glass full of ice
Raspberry Liqueur	1/2 oz.	Shake and strain into a martini glass
Pineapple Juice	2 oz.	Slowly add the raspberry liqueur down the side of the glass
Lemon Twist	1 each	Garnish with a twist

PRESS

Ingredients	Amounts	Preparation
Bucket Glass	6 - 10 oz.	Serving glass
Vodka or Gin or Bourbon	1 1/2 oz.	There is a choice of liquor in this cocktail
Ginger Ale	1 1/4 oz.	Build the drink directly into the serving glass
Soda Water	1 1/4 oz.	
Fresh Lemon Wedge	1 each	Garnish with a lemon wedge

RUM RUNNER

Ingredients	Amounts	Preparation
Highball Glass	6 - 10 oz.	Serving glass *Pre-chilled*
Light Rum	1 oz.	Build the cocktail into a mixing glass full of ice
Lime Juice	1/2 lime, squeezed	Pour all ingredients in
Pineapple Juice	3 oz.	Shake vigorously
Sugar Bitters	1 Tsp. 1 Dash	Pour into your highball serving glass
Dark Rum	1 oz.	Float dark rum here
Orange & a Cherry	1 each	Garnish with an orange & a cherry

ROB ROY

Ingredients	Amounts	Preparation
Martini Glass	6 - 10 oz.	Serving glass *Pre-chilled*
Scotch	3 oz.	Pour the scotch & vermouth into a mixing glass full of ice
Sweet Vermouth *Dry Vermouth	1 splash 1 Splash	Shake & strain into a martini glass
Lemon Twist	1 each	
*Perfect	*Pour both sweet & dry vermouth	If drink is specified as 'perfect', use both vermouths

RUSTY NAIL

Ingredients	Amounts	Preparation
Rocks Glass	6 - 8 oz.	Serving glass
Scotch	1 1/2 oz.	Build the cocktail directly into the serving glass
Drambui®	1 1/2 oz.	Full of ice
		No garnish

SALTY DOG

Ingredients	Amounts	Preparation
Highball Glass	12 oz.	Serving glass
Vodka	1 1/2 oz.	Build the cocktail directly into the serving glass
Grapefruit Juice	3 oz.	Full of ice
Kosher Salt		Use a 'salt rimmed' glass
Lime	1 each	Garnish with a lime wedge

SCOOBY SNACK

Ingredients	Amounts	Preparation
Rocks Glass *or Shot Glass	6 - 8 oz.	Serving glass
Coconut Rum	1/2 oz.	Build the cocktail into a mixing glass full of ice
Melon Liqueur	1/2 oz.	Shake & strain into a shot glass or pour over the rocks
Pineapple Juice	1/2 oz.	Unbelievably good!
Half & Half	1/2 oz.	

SCREWDRIVER

Ingredients	Amounts	Preparation
Highball Glass	12 oz.	Serving glass
Vodka	1 1/2 oz.	Build the cocktail directly into the serving glass
Orange Juice	4 oz.	Full of ice
Orange Wedge	1 each	Garnish with an orange wedge

SEA BREEZE

Ingredients	Amounts	Preparation
Highball Glass	12 oz.	Serving glass
Vodka	1 1/2 oz.	Build the cocktail directly into the serving glass
Grapefruit Juice	3 oz.	Full of ice
Cranberry Juice	1 splash	Splash for color at the end
Lime Wedge		Don't mix! It should look like a swirl!
		Garnish with a lime wedge

SEX ON THE BEACH

Ingredients	Amounts	Preparation
Bucket Glass	6 - 8 oz.	Serving glass
Vodka	1 1/2 oz.	
Peach Schnapps Orange Juice	1/4 oz. 2 oz.	Build the cocktail into the serving glass
Cranberry Juice	1/2 oz.	Full of ice
Lime Wedge		Garnish with a lime wedge

SIDE CAR

Ingredients	Amounts	Preparation
Martini Glass	6 - 10 oz.	Serving glass *Pre-chilled*
Brandy	2 1/2 oz.	Pour brandy, triple sec, lemon juice & lemon squeezes
Triple Sec	1/2 oz.	Into a mixing glass full of ice
Fresh Lemon Juice Lemon Wedges	3/4 oz. 6 Each	Shake & strain into a sugar rimmed, chilled, martini glass
Lemon Twist	1 Each	Garnish with a lemon twist

SINGAPORE SLING

Ingredients	Amounts	Preparation
Highball Glass	12 oz.	Serving glass
Gin	1 oz.	Build all ingredi-ents directly into the serving glass
Cherry Brandy	1/2 oz.	Full of ice
Sweet & Sour	1 1/2 oz.	In the order listed
Soda Water	1 1/2 oz.	
Cherry and a Lemon Wedge	1 each	Garnish with a cherry and a wedge of lemon

SLOE COMFORTABLE SCREW

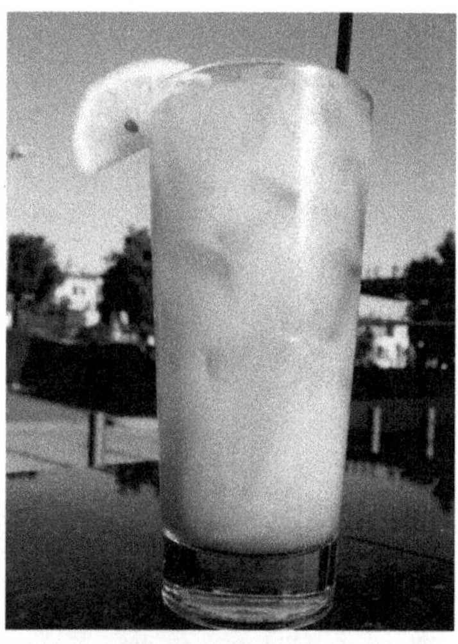

Ingredients	Amounts	Preparation
Highball Glass	12 oz.	Serving glass
Vodka	1 1/2 oz.	Build directly into the serving glass
Sloe Gin	1/2 oz.	Add the ingredients
Orange Juice	4 oz.	In the order listed
Lemon Wedge	1 each	Garnish with a lemon wedge

SMITH & KERNS

Ingredients	Amounts	Preparation
Highball Glass	12 oz.	Serving glass
Vodka	3/4 oz.	Build ingredients directly into the serving glass
Coffee Liqueur	3/4 oz.	Full of ice
Half & Half	1 1/2 oz.	Cream will work
Soda Water	fill glass	Float soda on top

SPRITZER

Ingredients	Amounts	Preparation
Wine Goblet	14 - 20 oz.	Serving glass
White Wine	4 oz.	Fill large wine glass with ice
Soda Water	2 oz.	Add wine then soda
*Lemon Lime Soda		*Optional
Lemon Wedge	1 each	On the rim

STINGER

Ingredients	Amounts	Preparation
Rocks Glass	6 - 8 oz.	Serving glass
Brandy	1 1/2 oz.	Build ingredients directly into the rocks serving glass
White Crème de Menthe	1 1/2 oz.	Full of ice
		No garnish

SUMMER HUMMER

Ingredients	Amounts	Preparation
Martini Glass	6 - 10 oz.	Serving glass *Pre-chilled*
Vodka	2 oz.	Pour the vodka, peach schnapps, triple sec & lemonade into a mixing glass
Peach Schnapps	1/4 oz.	Full of ice
Triple Sec Lemonade	3/4 oz. 2 oz.	Shake & strain into a chilled, sugar rimmed martini glass
Grenadine Sugar Rim	1 splash	Pour grenadine slowly down the inside of the glass
Lemon Wedge	1 each	Garnish with a lemon wedge

SURFER ON ACID

Ingredients	Amounts	Preparation
Rocks Glass	6 - 8 oz.	Serving glass
Coconut Rum	3/4 oz.	Build the ingredients directly into the rocks serving glass
Jagermeister®	3/4 oz.	Full of ice
Pineapple Juice	1 oz.	No garnish
*or as a Shot		If it's a shot, build into a mixing glass, shake & strain into a shot glass

TEQUILA SUNRISE

Ingredients	Amounts	Preparation
Highball Glass	12 oz.	Serving glass
Tequila	1 1/2 oz.	Build the tequila & orange juice into the serving glass
Orange Juice	4 oz.	Full of ice
Grenadine	1 oz.	Slowly pour the grenadine down the inside of the glass
Orange Cherry	1 each 1 Each	Garnish with a cherry and an orange wedge

TOM COLLINS

Ingredients	Amounts	Preparation
Highball Glass	12 oz.	Serving glass
Gin	1 1/2 oz.	Build drink Into a mixing glass full of ice
Sweet & Sour	3 oz.	Shake vigorously
Soda Water	1 oz.	Create a froth
Squeeze of Lime Orange & Lemon	1 each	Pour everything into the highball serving glass
		Garnish with lemon & a cherry

VESPER

Ingredients	Amounts	Preparation
Martini Glass	6 - 10 oz.	Serving glass *Pre-chilled*
Gin	1 1/2 oz.	Pour gin, vodka and vermouth into a mixing glass full of ice
Vodka	1/2 oz.	Shake vigorously. Let 'cure' for 10 seconds
'Dry' Vermouth or Chablis	1/4 oz. or less	Strain into a martini glass
Lemon Twist	1 each	Garnish with a twist

VODKA COLLINS

Ingredients	Amounts	Preparation
Highball Glass	12 oz.	Serving glass
Vodka	1 1/2 oz.	Build drink into a mixing glass full of ice
Sweet & Sour	3 oz.	Shake vigorously
Soda Water	1 oz.	Create a froth
Squeeze of Lime, Orange & Lemon	1 each	Pour into the serving glass
Orange & Cherry		Garnish with orange and a cherry

WHISKEY SOUR

Ingredients	Amounts	Preparation
Bucket Glass	10 - 12 oz.	Serving glass
Bourbon Whiskey	1 1/2 oz.	Build the bourbon and fresh sweet & sour into a mixing glass, with ice
Sweet & Sour Lemon Squeeze	3 oz. 1 each	Then squeeze your lemon, orange and lime wedges
Lime Squeeze Orange Squeeze	1 each 1 each	Shake and pour everything into your serving glass
Cherry Orange Wedge	1 each	Garnish with an orange and a cherry

WHITE RUSSIAN

Ingredients	Amounts	Preparation
Rocks Glass	6 - 8 oz.	Serving glass
Russian Vodka	1 1/2 oz.	Build the ingredients directly into the serving glass
Coffee Liqueur	1 1/2 oz.	Full of ice
Half & Half	1 oz.	Don't mix

WINE COOLER

Ingredients	Amounts	Preparation
Red Wine Goblet	14 - 20 oz.	Serving glass
Red Wine	4 oz.	Begin with a large wine serving glass full of ice
Lemon Lime Soda	2 oz.	Add wine then the lemon lime soda
*Soda Water		*Optional
Lemon Twist	1 each	

WOO WOO

Ingredients	Amounts	Preparation
Martini Glass	6 - 10 oz.	Serving glass *Pre-chilled*
Vodka	1 1/2 oz.	Pour all the ingredients
Peach Schnapps	1/2 oz.	Over ice in a mixing glass
Cranberry Juice	2 oz.	Shake and strain into a chilled martini glass
Lemon Twist	1 each	Garnish with a twist

57 CHEVY

Ingredients	Amounts	Preparation
Highball Glass	12 oz.	Serving class
Southern Comfort ®	1 oz.	Build all ingredients
Vodka	1/2 oz.	Into the serving glass
Grand Marnier	1/2 oz.	Full of ice
Pineapple Juice	2 oz.	
Cherry	1 each	Garnish with a cherry

Cocktails...

The drinks on the preceding pages are designed to be poured "free-hand." The laws and ABC regulations here in the states are such that we, as bartenders, are allowed to use this "freehand" technique to pour our drinks. This means without a measuring cup. Not every country allows this true luxury. In England for example... "every dram" is carefully measured "by law." The "art of the cocktail" is as much the preparation as it is the presentation, in addition to the taste and texture, of course. But the whole journey should be based in fun. Try to engage your guests. Perhaps a joke... a bar trick? Maybe they just want to be left alone. You have to be able to gauge what your guest wants.
Try to anticipate. The final goal is happy guests... right? How you achieve this is a glorious journey. So... have fun, be your-self and most importantly, be safe!

Chapter 6
Bar Jokes

They're just jokes...

This book is in no way intended to hurt, humiliate, intimidate, belittle or cause harm to anyone in any way!

This guide began as a collection of cocktail napkins, upon which I had jotted down the funny jokes that I hear. I was literally brining a shoebox full of jokes to work everyday.

These jokes are ones that the author has heard from behind the bar, over the course of many, many years. A good one, of course, is in the listener's ear and the delivery. Such a subjective topic... What is funny? Well... that's hard to define. The true origins of these jokes would be impossible to pinpoint. Their original authors are somewhere out there, lost along the way. This book is meant to bring joy and laughter to those who share in it. It is NOT intended to cause discomfort to those that may find some of its content offensive.

To those people... I am sorry.

So This Guy Walks Into A Bar

- Horse walks into a bar..........
  .... Bartender says
  "Why the long face?"

- Ham sandwich walks into a bar,
  ....Bartender says
  "We don't serve food here."

- Termite walks into a bar and
  says........."Where's the bar tender?"

- This guy walks into a bar with some jumper
  cables. He orders a beer.
  The bartender says "OK..................
  But don't start anything!"

- What did the giraffe say when
  he went into the bar? ....
  ..."High Balls on me!"

Another Guy Walks Into A Bar....

- This gigantic polar bear walks into a bar and he says........ .... "I'll have a beer," and the bartender says, "sure, but why the long pause?" Polar Bear says "I was born that way."

- So this Japanese guy walks into a bar and orders a 'Stoli with a Twist'..... ....The bartender says..."Okay, so there were these four little pigs."

- This Grasshopper goes into a bar........... The bartender says, "Hey!... We have a drink named after you." The grasshopper says, "Who would want a drink named Bob"?

- So this Penguin goes into a bar. He says to the bartender "Did you see my brother in here earlier? ....Bartender Says, "What does he look like?"

Clean Jokes....(Short Chapter)

- Why was six afraid of seven?
  ....
  ....Because seven ate nine.

- What did the ocean say to the shore?
  ....Nothing, she just waved.

- What do you get when you cross a pig with a chicken?..................Ham & Eggs.

- Did you hear the one about the tractor salesman's wife who wrote him a John Deere Letter?

- Two peanuts were walking down the street..........
  ....One was assaulted.

Clean Jokes

- What did the '0' say to the '8' ?
  .... "Nice belt."

- Did you hear what the pony said when he had a sore throat?...... "I'm a little horse."

- There was this terrible accident between two turtles. The only witness was a snail. So when the cops showed up and asked the snail what happened ....
  The snail says, "I don't know man. It all happened so fast."

- What is the most potent food to kill your sex drive?...................Wedding Cake!

- What did the Dalai Lama say to the hot dog vendor?...........
  "Make me one with everything."

More Clean Jokes

- So this guy is in a bar alone, having a beer.

Out of nowhere he hears "Hey buddy... nice tie!" He looks around, doesn't see anyone, and decides he must be hearing things. After a little while, he hears a little voice again... "Hey you...nice shirt." To this guy's amazement, there is still nobody within 25 feet of him. He is baffled. So he calls the bartender down and asks him. "Have you been hearing voices?... There's this little voice that keeps telling me how nice my tie is."
The bartender says... "Oh yeah,... that happens all the time, it's the complimentary peanuts."

- An 80 year old guy takes confession. He goes in and says, "Father, I am 80 years old, and I have been married for 50 years and never cheated on my wife, until last night. Last night, I made love to two 18 year old girls, all night long."

"My goodness my son, this is shocking...
How long has it been since you have given confession?" "Never!" the man replied............
"I'm Jewish... I'm just telling everyone."

Quickies

- So there were these two cannibals eating a clown, one of them turns to the other and says..............................
…"Does this taste funny to you?"

- Did you hear about the new experimental breakfast cereal for impotent men?..
It's called... Nut & Raisin Honey.

- Why don't blind people sky dive?… ....
.......It scares the hell out of the dog.

- Why is divorce so expensive?
.... It's worth it.

- Did you hear about the midget, psychic escaped convict?...

He was a Small Medium at Large.

More Quickies

- How do you know you have been robbed by an Asian?......................You get home and your dog is gone but your kid's homework is finished.

- Did you hear about the new 'Divorced' Barbie Doll?.........
It comes with all of Ken's stuff.

- Why don't Amish folks make love standing up?...........It could lead to dancing.

- Three old guys are walking... first one says, "It's windy isn't it?" The second guy says, "No it's Thursday." Third guy says, "Me too, lets go get a beer."

- If there are flies in the kitchen... Which one is the cowboy?..................................
....The one on the range.

Even More Quickies

- How can you tell when a lawyer is lying? ....His lips are moving.

- What is Mickey Mantle's least favorite inning? ....Bottom of the Fifth.

- What is the perfect breakfast?............ Your son is on the box of Wheatties, your mistress is on the cover of Playboy and your wife is on the back of a milk carton.

- Why does a mushroom make a good date? ....Because he is a 'Fungi.'

- Did you hear about the gay midget?............ He came out of the cupboard.

A Few More Quickies

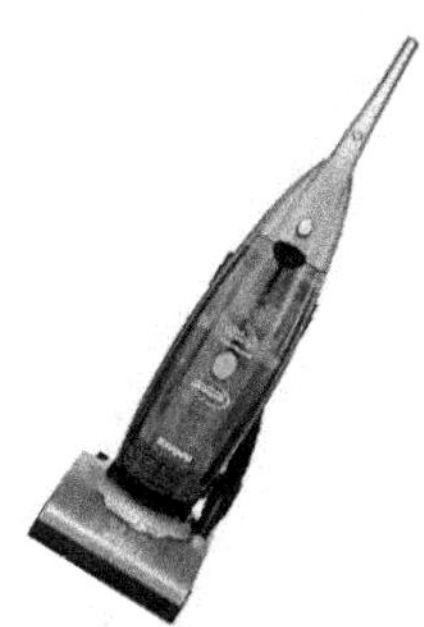

- What's the difference between a Hoover and a Harley?.......
  Position of the dirt bag.

- Father walks into his son's room and catches him playing with himself.... Dad says "Don't do that son, it will make you go blind".........His son says... "Dad!... I'm over here."

- Why is sex a lot like air?.................. Because it's no big deal, until you're not getting any.

- What does Bill Clinton say to his wife after sex?...................
  "I'll be home in an hour."

- What do Viagra and Disneyland have in common?................You have to wait an hour for a two minute ride.

More Quickies

- This guy introduces himself to this girl and she says her name is 'Carmen,' he replies, "That's a nice name, where does it come from?"...........She says "It represents the two most important things in life to me... Cars and Men," "What's your name?" she says.... "Beer Sex", he replies...

- Did you hear about the couple on their first date, kissing on her front porch? He says "Are you going to invite me up?"..... She says "No... I don't do that on the first date." He says, "How about the last date?"

- Husband and wife discover an "S & M" magazine in their son's room. Wife says "What are we going to do" ? Husband says, "Well, we certainly are not going to spank him."

Twisted Jokes

- A little old man shuffled very slowly into an ice cream parlor and painfully pulled himself up onto the stool. After catching his breath, he ordered a banana split. The waitress kindly asked, "Crushed nuts?" He says,... "No... arthritis."

- Doctor Dave had recently slept with one of his patients and he felt guilty about it. Really guilty. No matter how hard he tried to forget about it, his sense of wrongdoing and betrayal was overwhelming. But then he would hear a reassuring voice in his head say, "Dave... you know you're not the first doctor to sleep with one of his patients, don't worry about it, just let it go." Well then another voice in his head would bring him back to reality and say... Dave... Dave...Dave...
  .....You're a veterinarian.

- A young boy walks into a convenience store and puts a box of tampons on the counter. The man at the counter said, "Son, do you know what these are for?" The kid says "No, not exactly, but the TV says if you use these, you can swim and ride a bike and I can't do either."

Some More Twisted Jokes

- Why is there no Disneyland in China?.......
No one's tall enough to go on the good rides.
-
- What do you call a fish with no eyes?..................... **A fsh**

- Why do only 30% of women get into heaven?...
Because if it were any more, it would be hell.

- A blond girl is in a trivial pursuit game after rolling the dice, her question came up on "Science & Nature." The question was "If you are in a vacuum and someone calls your name... could you hear them?"................
She says, "Is it on or off?"

- Why does it take you <u>and</u> your girlfriend to screw in a light bulb?
.... It just DOES Dammit!

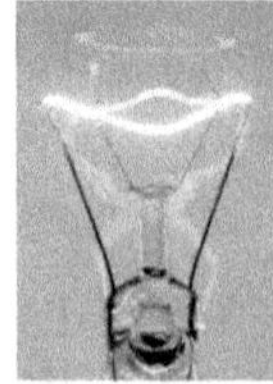

- One day... a long, long time ago... surprisingly there was this woman who did not whine, nag or bitch... but that was a long, long time ago, plus it was just one day.

Women Jokes

- How many feminists does it take to screw in a light bulb? ....That's not fair...
- Two lesbians in a bar.
  One says "Let me be frank with you,".........
  ....The other says,..."No let me!"
- What do you call 1000 lesbians with rifles? ....Militia Ethridge.
- What's the difference between a dog and a fox?............. Five drinks. .
- How many chauvinists does it take to screw in a light bulb?..................................
  ....None...let her sit in the dark.
- Did you hear about the Irish Lesbian?........... He preferred women over whiskey.

Blond Jokes

- A blond woman in a bar was bragging about her knowledge of state capitals. She says, "Go ahead, ask me… I know them all!" So the bartender says, "Ok, what's the capital of Wisconsin?"
  She says, "That's easy… 'W.'"

- Doctor asks his blond patient, "Are you sexually active?"……………………………… She says, "No… I just lie there."

- How do you paralyze a woman from the neck down?……………..…..Marry Her!

- How many blonds does it take to screw in a light bulb?……..One, she just holds the bulb and the world revolves around her.

More Blond Jokes

- This blond lady goes into the library, walks right up to the front desk and says, "I'd like a cheeseburger, fries and a diet coke."
  The librarian says, "I'm sorry, you must be mistaken… this is a library.
  The blond says, "oops, my bad, ***ssshhh! I'd like a cheeseburger, fries and a diet coke."***

- Two blonds, each standing on either shore of a river. One calls out, "hey...how do you get to the other side?" The other blond replies……
  "You're already on it!"

- How do you know a blond has been using your computer?
  There is white out on the screen.

Lawyer Jokes

- What is the difference between a lawyer and a vulture?............ Removable wingtips.

- What's the difference between a lawyer and a vampire?..
  A vampire only sucks blood at night.

- What do you get when you cross a pig and a lawyer?.....

  Nothing… there are some things even a pig won't do.

- If you came upon a lawyer and an IRS agent drowning…………………………………………..
  ……Would you read the paper or go to lunch?

- What do you call a lawyer buried up to his neck in sand?...
  Not enough sand.

More Lawyer Jokes

- What do you throw a drowning lawyer?....... His partners.

- What does a lawyer use for birth control?... Their personality.

- How many lawyers does it take to screw in a light bulb?...................Three… one to climb the ladder, one to shake the light bulb and one to sue the ladder company.

- What's the difference between a lawyer and a gigolo?.......... A gigolo only screws one person at a time.

- What do you call 50 lawyers at the bottom of the sea?......A good start.

- What's brown and black and looks good on a lawyer?…. …………..…. .A Doberman.

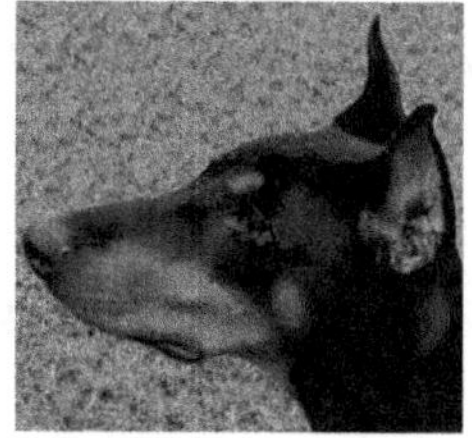

Man Jokes

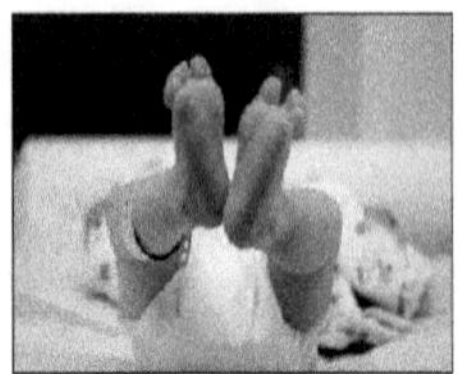

- Why is it dangerous to let a man's mind wander?........... It's too little to be out alone.

- Why do little boys whine?........................ They're practicing to be men.

- Why are guys different from government bonds? ....Bonds mature…

- What's the difference between a new husband and a new dog?…………………..…. After a year… the dog is still delighted to see you...

- Why is it so hard for a woman to find a caring, sensitive and good looking guy?................................. All those guys already have boyfriends.

Random Jokes

- What's the difference between a man and ET ? ....ET phoned home!

- What is a man's idea of a seven course meal? .... A hot dog and a six pack

- So this guy goes into his psychiatrist's office in glad wrap underwear......
  The shrink says, "Well, I can clearly see you're nuts."

- What do you do if your girlfriend starts smoking?...... Slow down and use a lubricant.

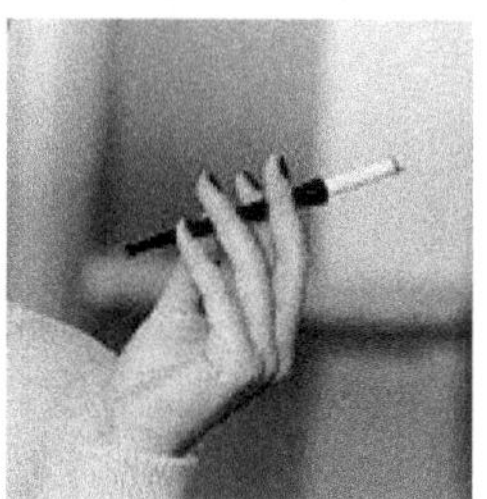

- Two hats were hanging on a hat rack in the hall. One of 'em says,...........................
  "You stay here... I'll go on a head."

More Random Jokes

- Why is a laundry mat a bad place to pick up women?.... Because if she can't afford her own washing machine, how is she going to support you?

- A female officer was arresting a man for drunk driving.... She says, "Anything you say, can and will be held against you."
  So he says..."Your breasts!"

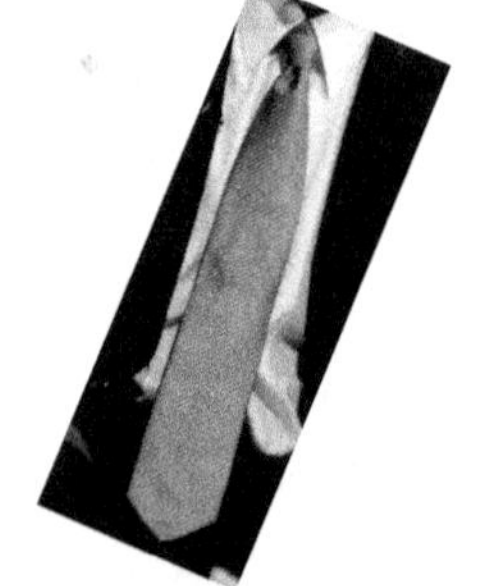

- Two silk worms had a race..... They ended in a tie.

- No matter how much you push the envelope..................................
  It will still be stationary.

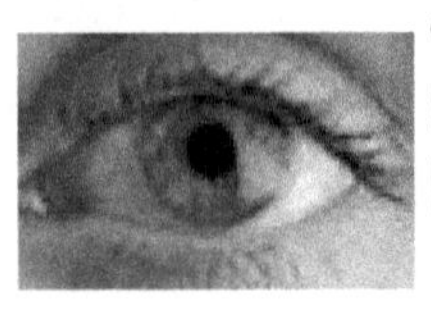

- Why do men find it difficult to make eye contact?.......... Because breasts don't have eyes.

Biker Joke

- A man dies and goes to heaven… He appears at the pearly gates and St. Peter says, "Have you ever done anything of particular merit?"……………….. The man replies, "I can think of one thing… Recently I came across a group of bikers who were bothering a pretty young woman. I told them to leave her alone, but they wouldn't listen. So I approached the biggest and meanest looking one. I kicked over his motorcycle, punched him in the mouth, ripped out his nose ring, threw it on the ground and stomped on it… Then I told him and his friends… 'Now get out of here.'"…. St. Peter was visibly impressed with this so he said… "I am quite impressed, my son, when did this happen?...."
  The man says… "Just a few minutes ago."

Don't Try This… This is very Dangerous!

Chapter 7
Bar Tricks

So What Exactly Is A Bar Trick?

The following pages represent a fine collection of activities and tricks, designed to entertain your guests. There are some serious bartender techniques, as well as some playful nonsense. Nonetheless... Entertainment is serious business! Good for you and good for the bar where you work. Happy and satisfied guests is my goal.

The bar tricks on the following pages have helped me make a lot of money over the course of the years. I took the initiative to "entertain" my guests. But be careful... When to do a bar trick is tricky. There is always work to be done and your workmates may not appreciate your "fooling around." Choose your time for entertaining carefully. Be a great host... If this is your goal... then you will succeed. Good Luck!

Why?

I ask this of myself often.

Oh, don't think you won't have your hecklers. These come in many forms. So… it's simple, really. It is an entertaining "break" from the monotony of the bar scene. Laughter is life. If I make people happy, it builds business, it keeps your tipping guests there longer and giving bigger tips. If you are good and lucky… people will talk about you. Come and "see" you. You could create a following. Love your guests and they will love you. The items listed in this book will delight "most" of the people you show them to. If a particular person doesn't care, move on to someone else looking for interaction.

Don't push this stuff on anyone. It's for fun!

Execution

Whatever you do...

Do not practice any tricks in front of your guests!

You should practice at home. Do your tricks over and over again until you feel comfortable.

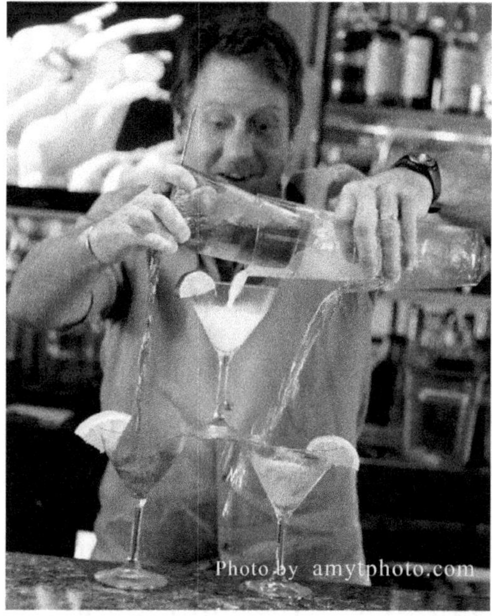

You should know what will happen and when, and in turn know what to expect next. This anticipation will make you look like a pro. If your trick fails, there lies the possibility of embarrassment. That's okay. Laugh it off… no matter what happens…Just have fun! Don't take any of this too seriously. The point is fun for you, and your guests.

Timing...

As in the previous page, know what to

expect, and when, concerning these activities. It will only make you look better... more professional. There is a time to break out a good trick and a time to get to work. To know the difference is the key. Many bartenders make the mistake of showing off or making friends when there are other duties to be done. Be aware... know your surroundings. Be in tune with what is going on around you and react to it accordingly. Do not force your partner or teammates to work harder while you play with the guests. This stuff is for creating something memorable. This could be jeopardized if the basic service is let down. Just be aware.

Know when to say fun.

Never Reveal Your Secrets

After every trick people are going to ask you…

"How did you do that?"

Never Tell them!

Just say… "It's like magic.

A magician never tells."

That's the rule…

Why should you?

This isn't rocket science…

It really doesn't matter, but why spoil the illusion? You don't need to diminish the moment. Just live the glory of your guest's joy. That's what you set out to achieve anyway. Bask in that and move on. Don't tell… It's never as interesting as the mystique. Unless you can sell it in a book, like me.

Perfect Lemon Twists

The thing about a good twist is the oil in the lemon rind or the skin. This is where the flavor lies. Here is a demonstration of how to make proper traditional lemon twists.

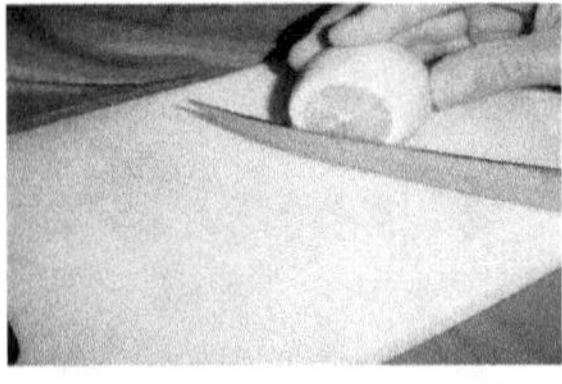

Ok… You begin with a nice firm lemon. Cut the ends off 'flat'. Then use an 'ice pick', spindle, or any other straight pointy thing, that will 'score' the white part of the lemon rind, go only halfway, turn the lemon around, score it from this other side.
This will separate the rind from the lemon. Slice the lemon. Cut one side & peel the twists away from the lemon.

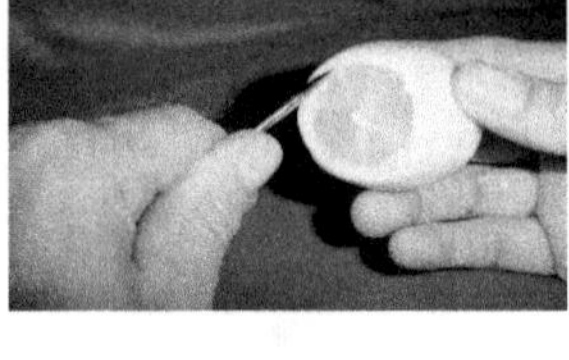

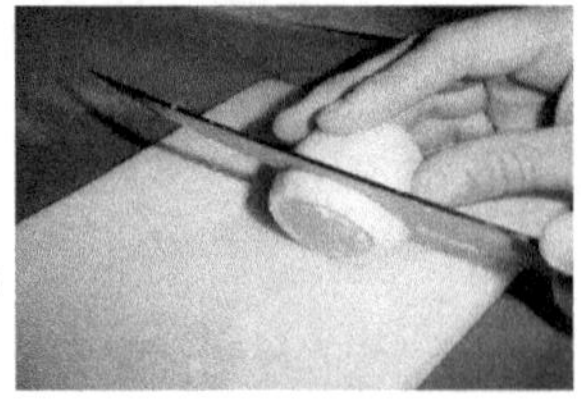

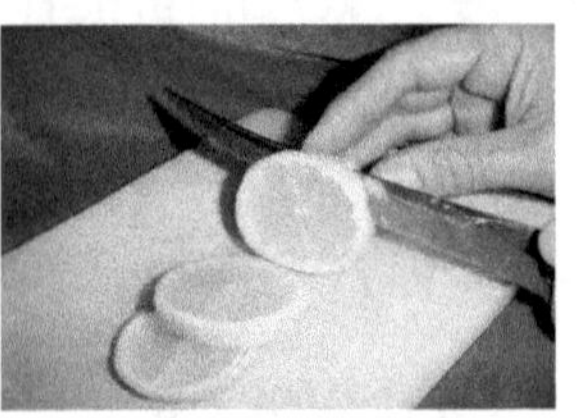

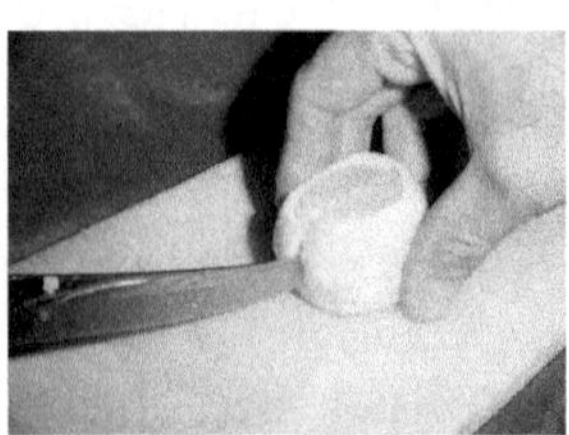

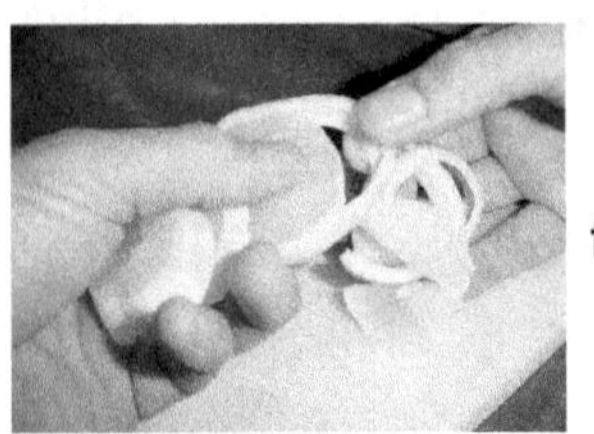

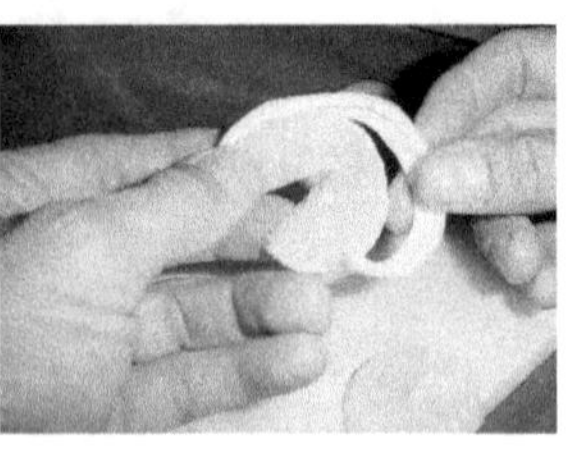

Perfect Lemon Twists

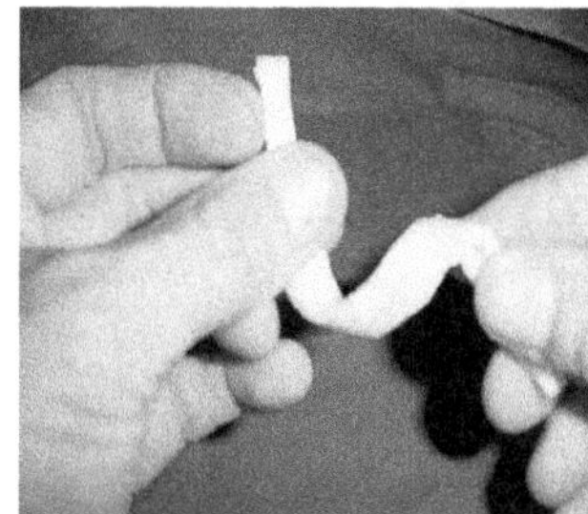

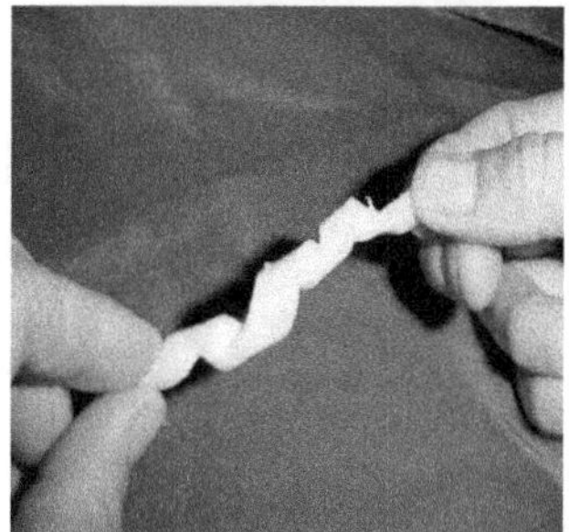

A twist is not a twist until you twist it... This will extract the essential oils out of the rind. Twist it tight... it should form sort of a pigs tail.

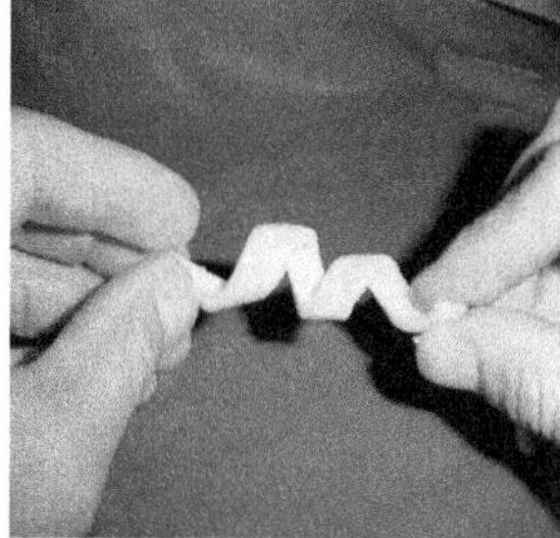

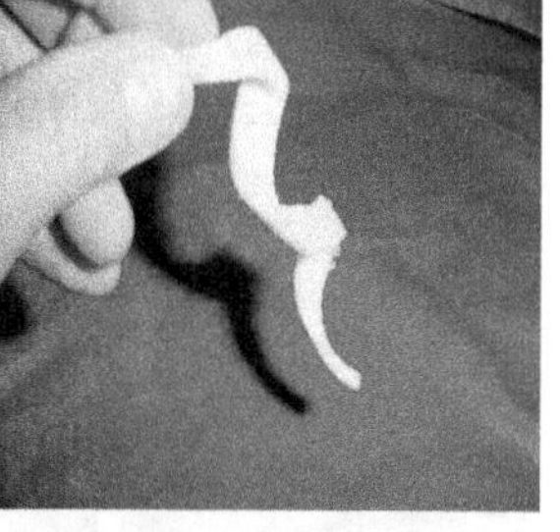

Blue Cheese Filled Black Olives

This is a tasty treat, in a Martini. Vodka or Gin, this flavorful garnish is a sure fire way to show your guests how much you love them.

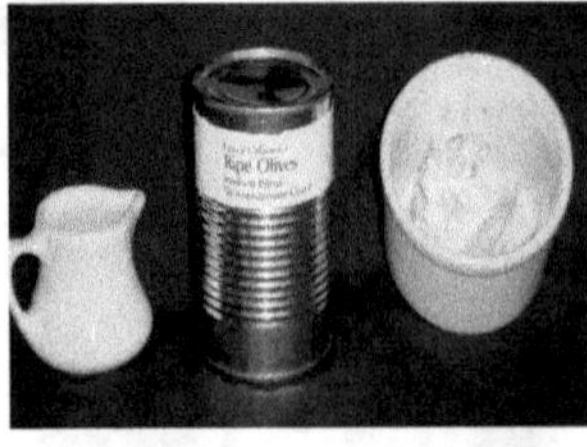

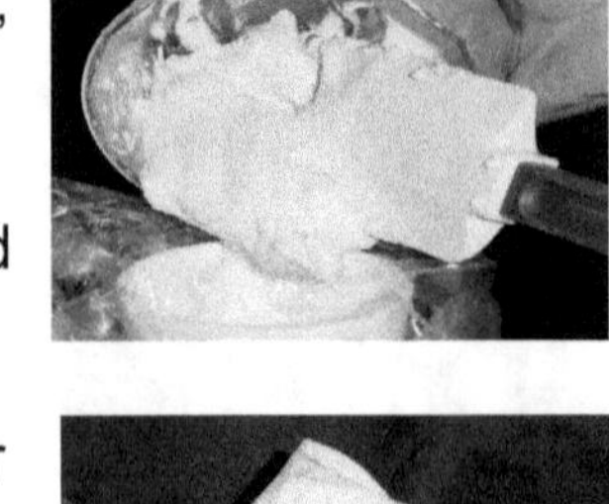

Begin with a can of 'pitted' black olives, blue cheese crumbles and cream. Crack some black pepper in there and whip in a food processor until smooth and creamy. Spatula this mix into a small plastic 'pastry' bag. Cut the corner off the bag and squirt the mixture into the black olives. Rinse the olives first.

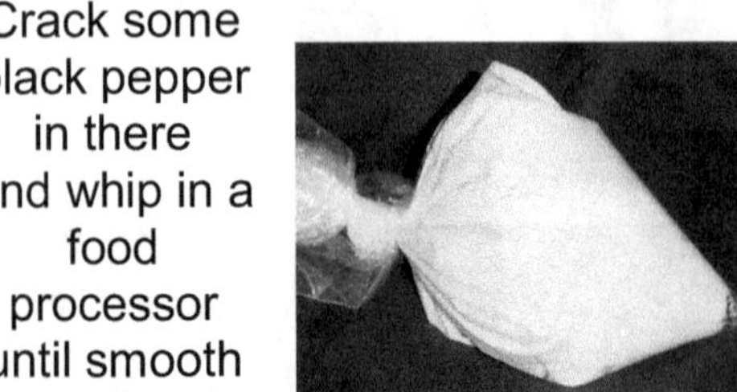

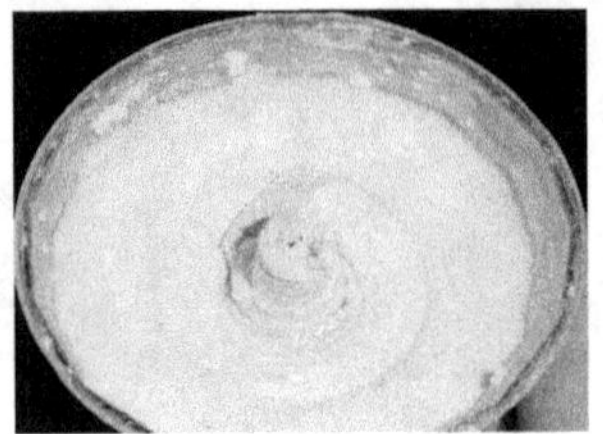

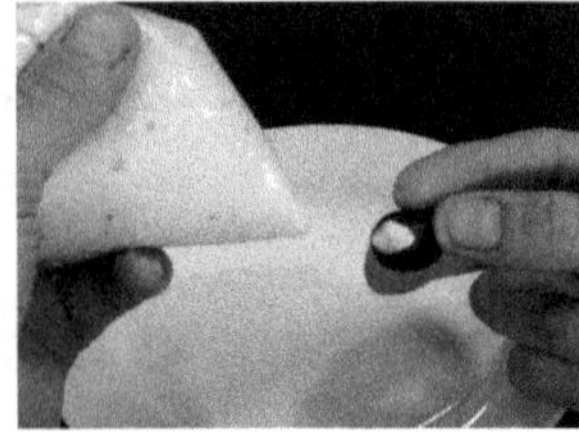

Blue Cheese Filled Black Olives

Make the whole can's worth of olives if you want. They'll go fast. Put on a pick and serve with your favorite martini.

World Greatest Hiccup Cure...

Really, it Works....
Try It...You'll See...

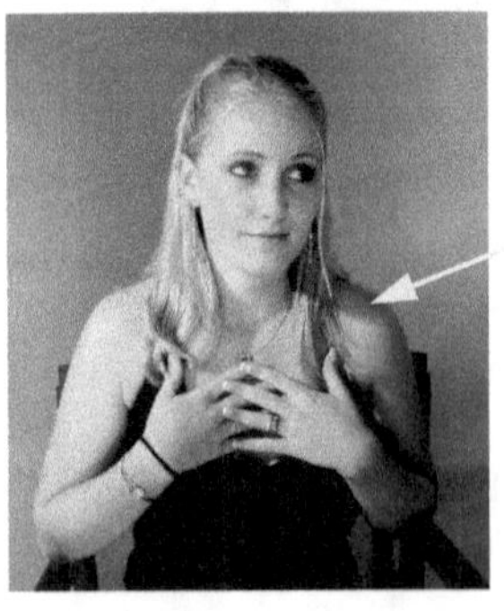

First...you need someone with the hiccups. A glass of water and a fairly large spoon.

Hold the spoon like this...

Place the Spoon, upside down in a small glass of water

World Greatest Hiccup Cure...

Drink the water while holding the bottom of the spoon in the water and pressing the scoop side of the spoon against your temple, drink the whole glass of water...

It Works!
Now this is a happy person that has been cured of the hiccups. Happy, Happy, Happy
Really...It Works!
This Is Jen...
Happy Jen..

Think of a Number...

Think of a number from two to ten…

But don't tell me.

Multiply that number by nine…

This gives you a two digit number.

Add the digits together…

Subtract five from this number…

Take the alphabetical equivalent… like 1 = A, 2 = B. That number gives you a letter…

Think of a country that begins with this letter.

Take the last letter of this country's name… and think of an animal that begins with this letter…

Now take the last letter of this animal and think of a color that begins with this letter…

Are you thinking of an

Orange **K**angaroo in **D**enmark?

The Paper Rose...

The Paper Rose...

Here we are going to demonstrate how to make a Cocktail Rose...
Using a common bar napkin.

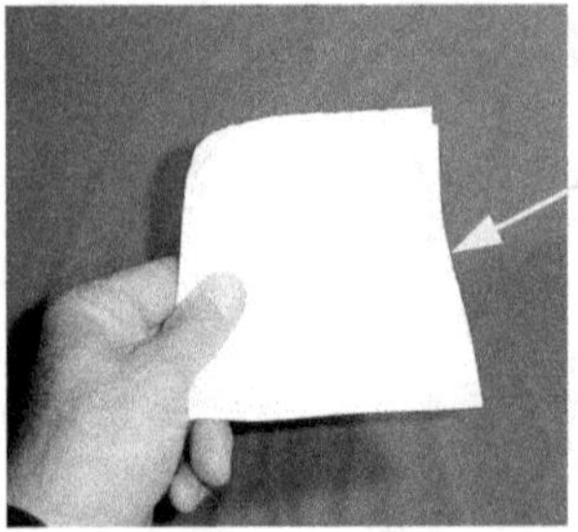

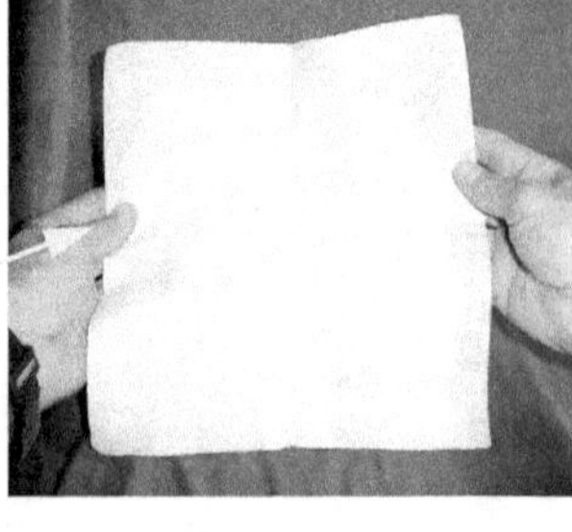

You will need a standard bar napkin. Sometimes called a 'Bev Nap'. Unfold it... Take one of the corners and begin to roll it up. Sort of scrunch it up as you go along. You don't want the petals to be too smooth. Roll the top all the way to the end evenly. See how I'm pinching in the top of the stem. Roll it tightly. Notice the corner of the napkin here. There will be two of them & they will become the leaves.

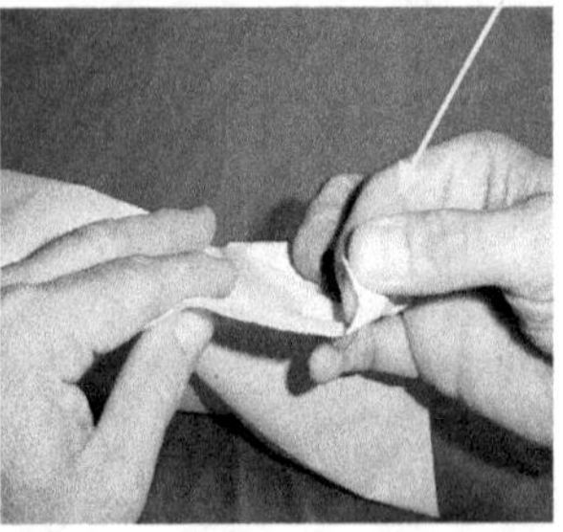

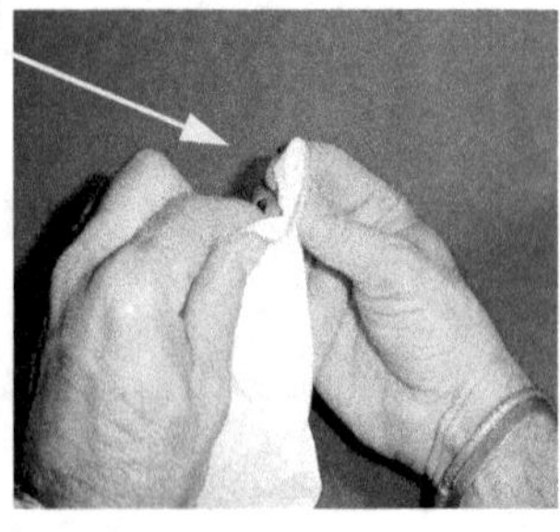

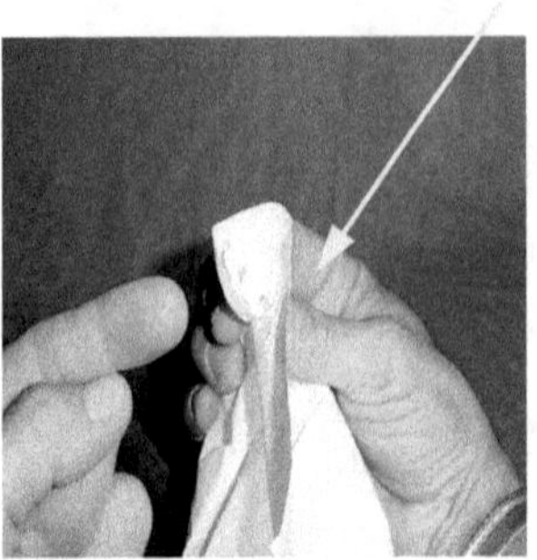

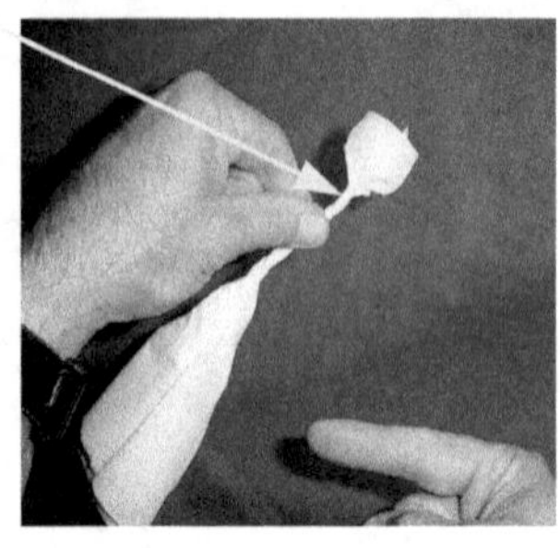

The Paper Rose

We've all seen it. Now you know how to do it.

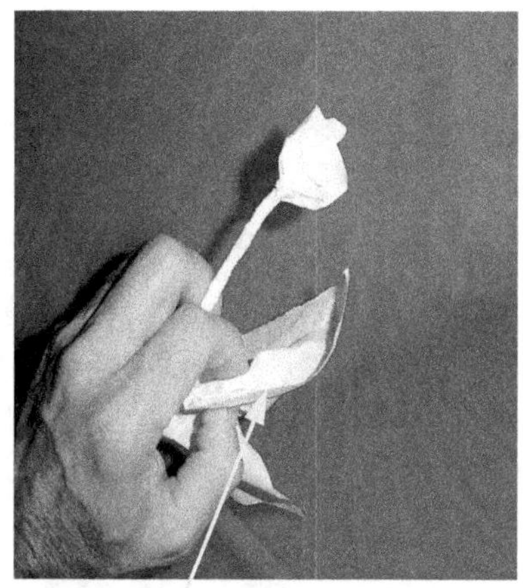

Okay…Spiral the stem all the way down. Very tightly. Peel the 'leaves', back up the stem. Here you go! You can singe the edges of the rose with fire.
Be careful, the paper burns quickly. Blow it out as soon as it begins to burn…and be careful!

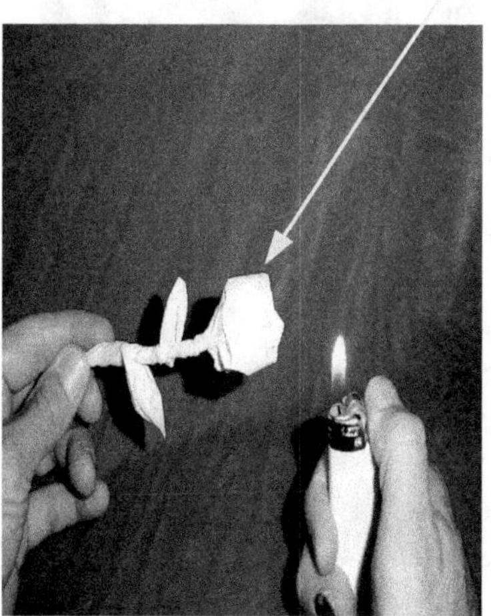

Martini Glass Decoration—Sugar

Gels & Sugars we call it… This demonstrates just another way for you to make your guest feel special. Color is key!

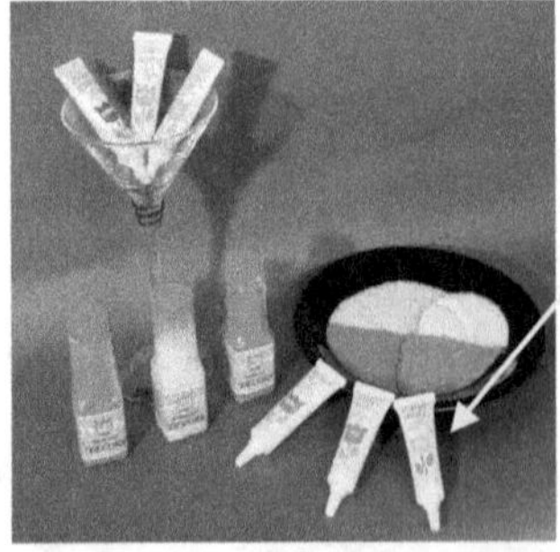

These 'Colored Sugars and Gels' are available in any supermarket, in the 'cake' section.

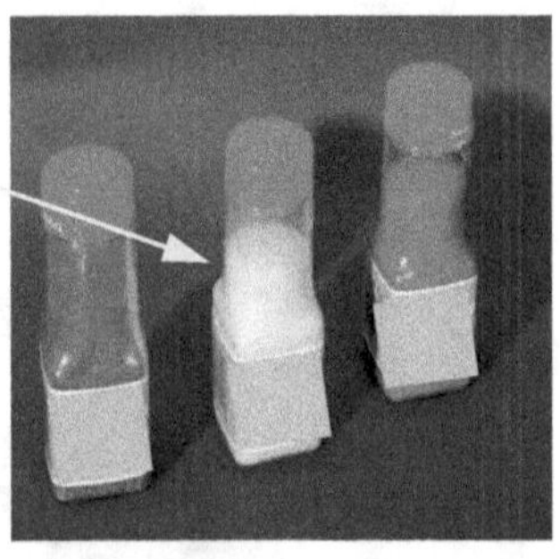

Sprinkle your 'colors' into your glass 'Rimmer'. A plate will do. Contrasting colors look the best. Gently shake the plate to spread the sugars.

Use a concentrated lime juice on the sponge. This works best to adhere the sugar to the glass.

Martini Glass Decoration—Sugar

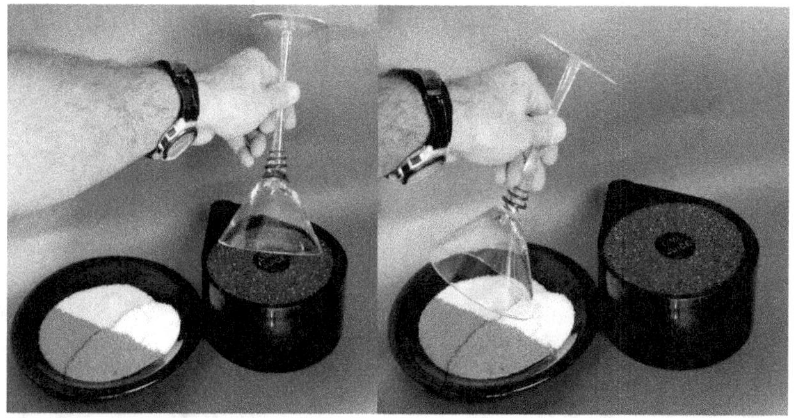

Dip the glass in the lime juice. Not too much... Just a nice even application. Then into the sugar. A rolling motion is best...

Now you've coated the rim with a colorful garnish and your glass is ready for its cocktail. Don't spill on the rim when you pour in the drink.

Just imagine the possibilities... Red white & blue for July 4th. Orange and black for Halloween. You get the picture... What's your favorite color? What's your favorite holiday? How about your country flag's colors?

Martini Glass Decoration—Gel

Swirl the gels on the inside of the glass and it will remain through this one cocktail. The chill of the drink keeps it on the side of the glass.

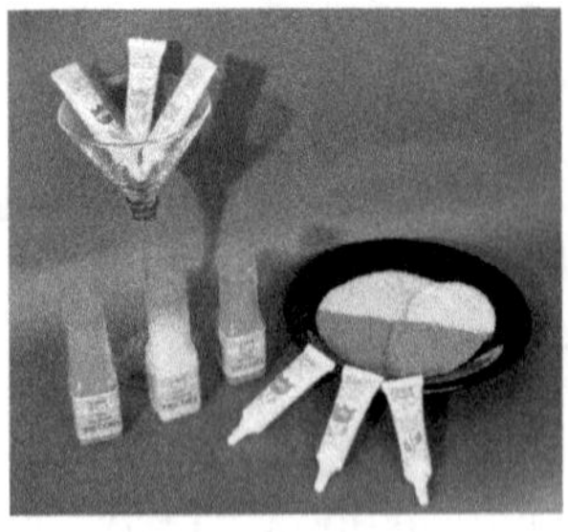

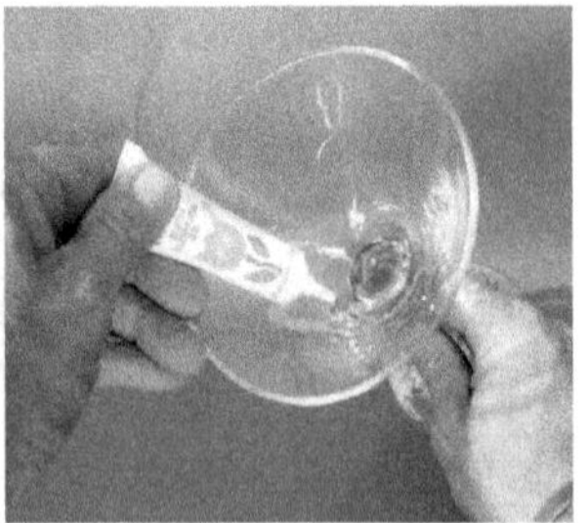

These Colored Gels are available in any supermarket, in the 'cake' section. 'Swirl' it around the inside of the glass...

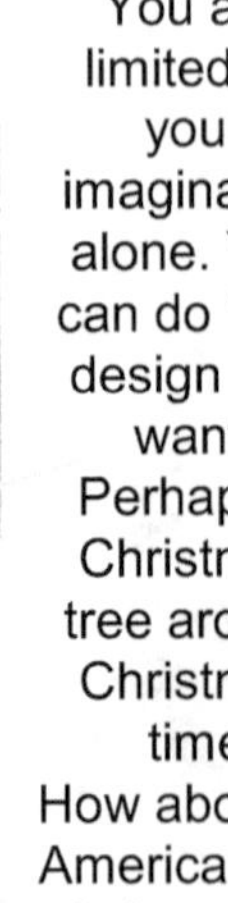

You are limited by your imagination alone. You can do 'any' design you want. Perhaps a Christmas tree around Christmas time How about an American flag in honor of our vets. **God Bless our Vets!**

Martini Glass Decoration—Chocolate

You will need a martini glass and a squeeze bottle of chocolate sauce. "Swirl this on the inside of the glass like so...

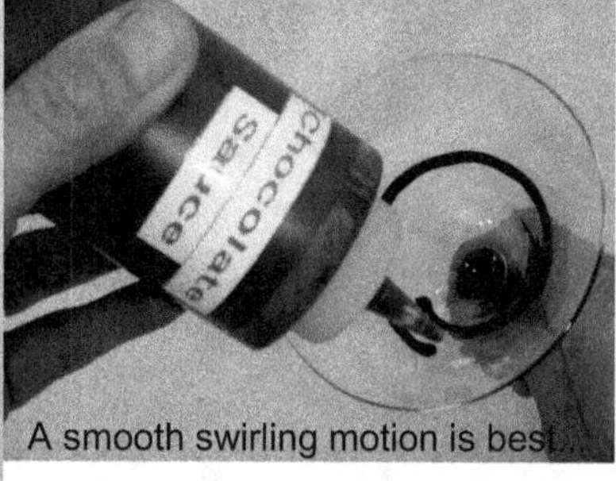

A smooth swirling motion is best...

Now you've got a chocolaty garnish. Looks cool doesn't it? Okay… Your glass is ready for its cocktail.

It doesn't have to be perfect, just personal...

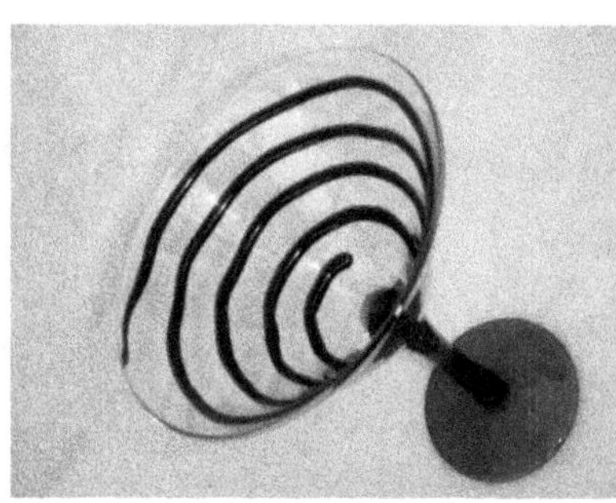

This one is for a Chocolate Martini

Wine Foil Vase

This is to show you the technique of how to make a miniature vase to hold an individual flower for a special guest.

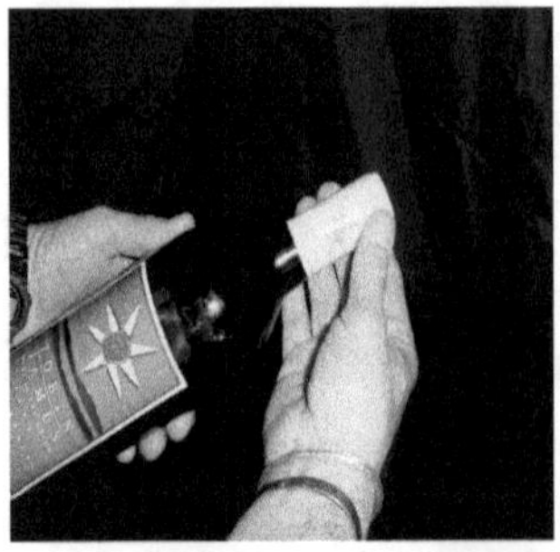

You'll need a wine foil, a quarter and a flower. Drop the quarter in the foil. It should fit perfectly. With the quarter at the bottom, begin to bend the foil in at about 2/3 from the open end. Use many small bends. The idea is to sort of creep the bends in. Turning as you go. While not crushing the center of the vase.

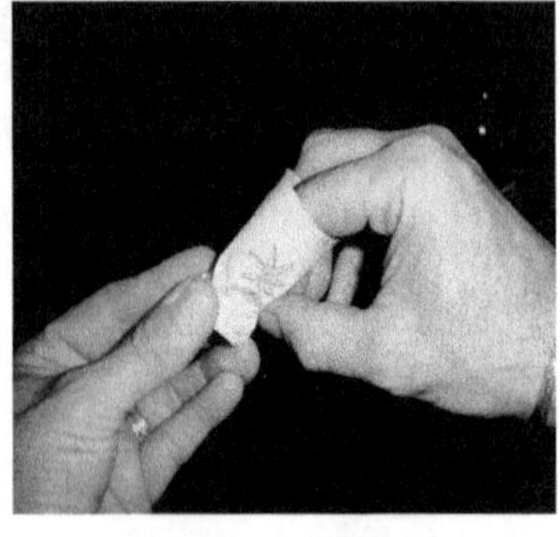

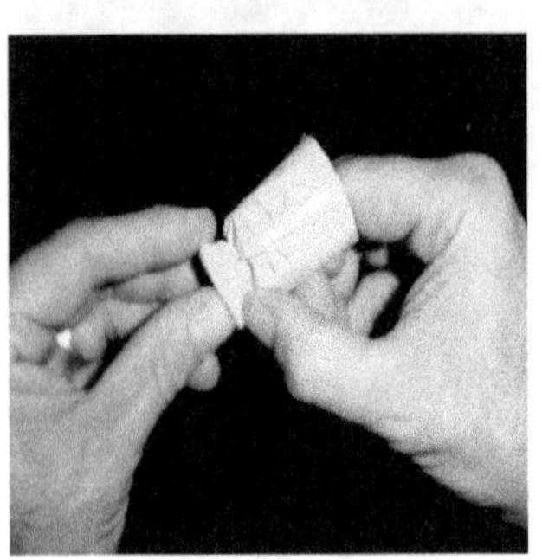

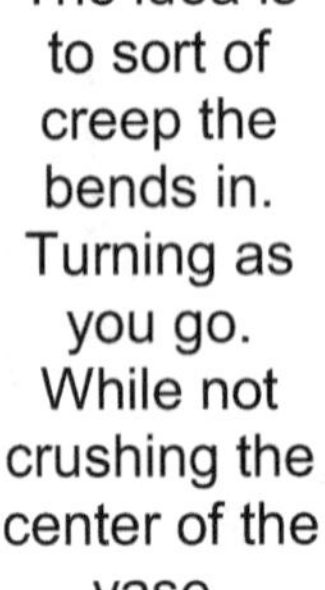

Wine Foil Vase

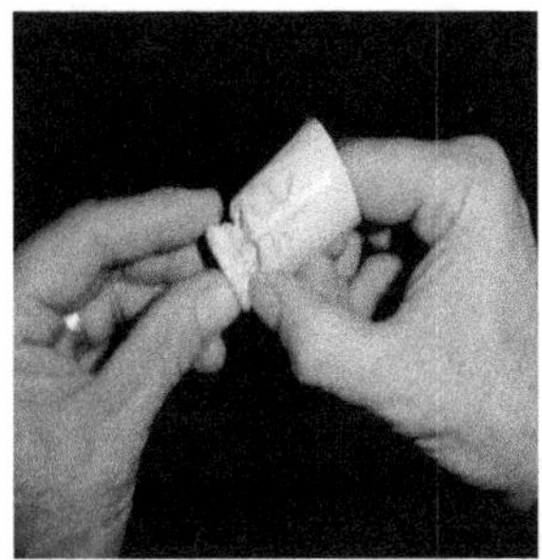

Keep working it in. Go all the way to the top, then leave a little flange. This will be the top of your vase. The top should be nice and round and so should the bottom. Place the vase firmly on a hard surface and make sure the bottom sits flat.

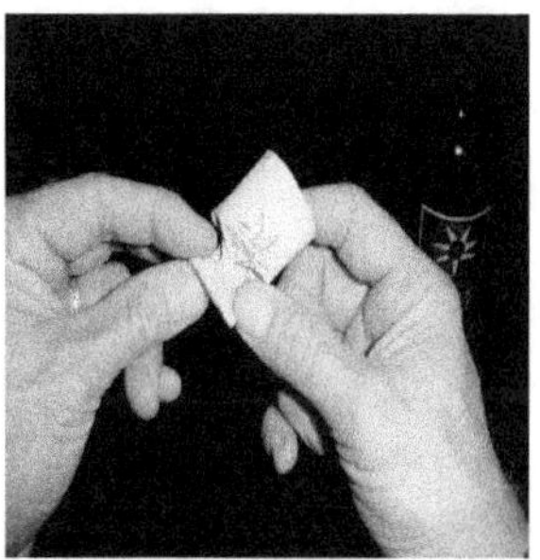

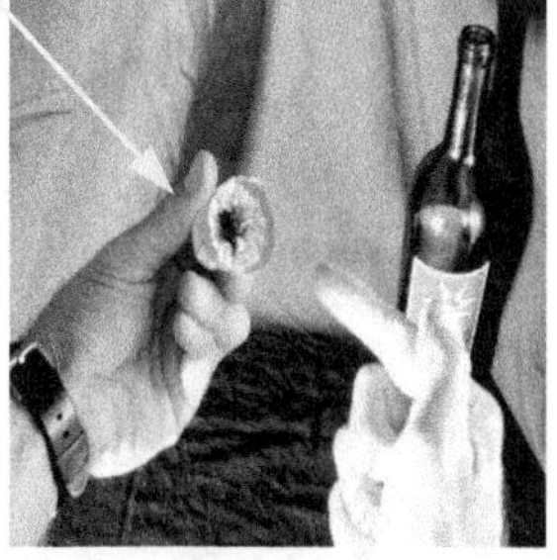

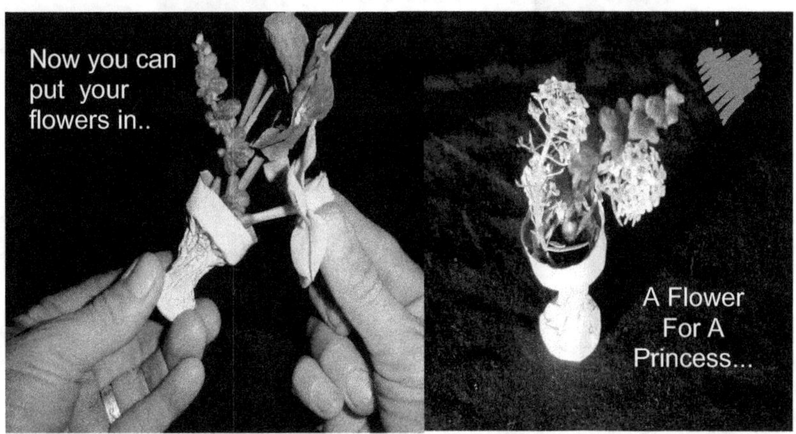

Candle on a Glass

This is just to show you the technique of attaching a candle to the rim of a glass.

Don't need much here. A glass, a candle and a lighter. Matches will work fine.

Drip a little of the wax on the edge of the glass. Then heat the other end of the candle with the lighter or match.

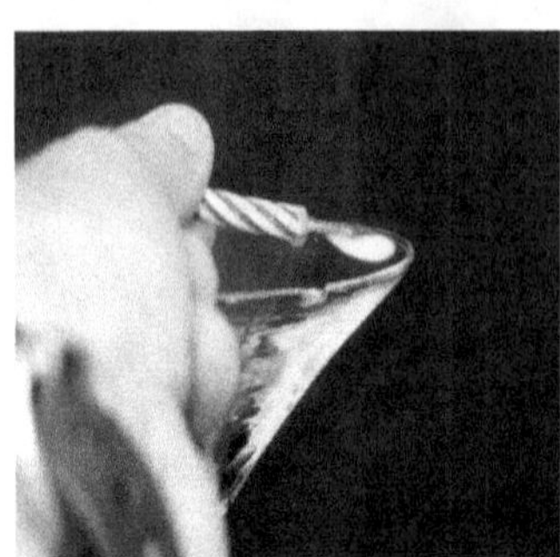

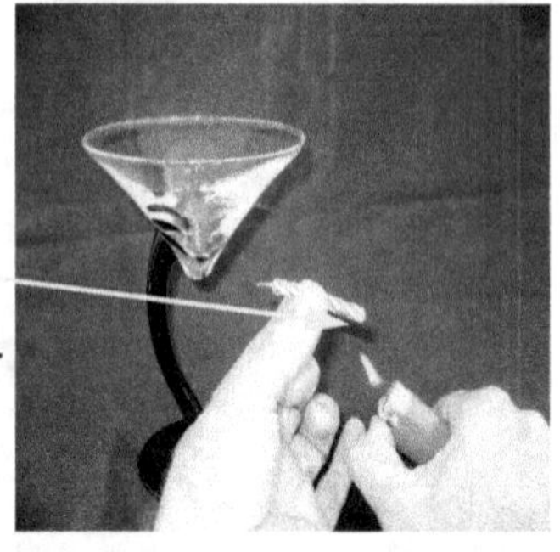

Push firmly down on the drip of wax. Take your fingers away quickly. Now you can pour the drink in the glass.

Birthday Glass

The idea is to make someone feel special.
This will do it every time...

Agent Orange

Here we are going to demonstrate how to carve an 'Agent Orange'

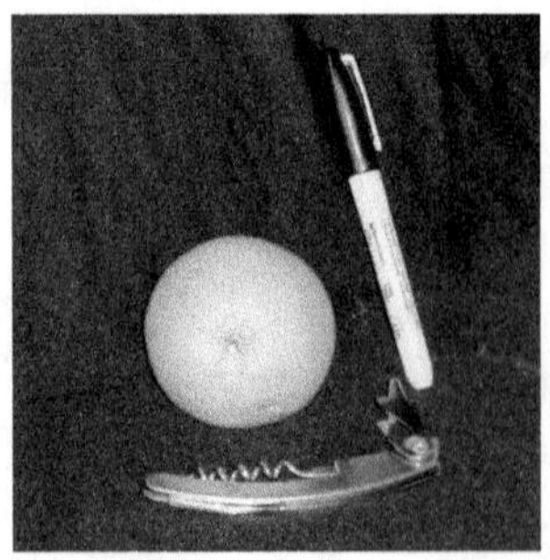

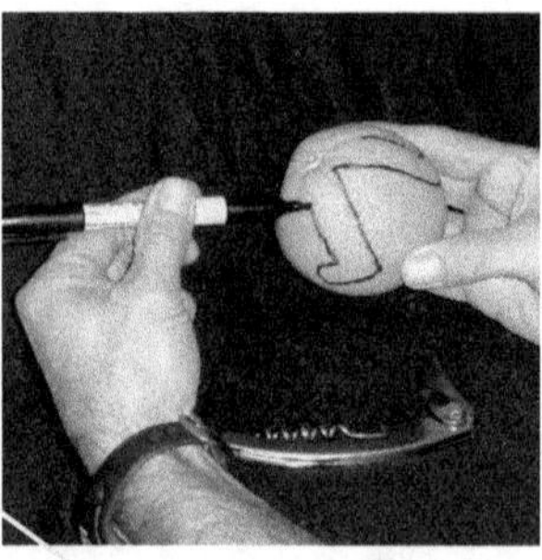

You'll need an orange, a pen and a knife. Draw the outline of a man on the outside of the orange. The 'navel' or the place where the stem attaches, this is his butt. Use the knife to carve along the edge of the figure. (Not too deep) Then... begin to peel the orange man away from the orange. When you get to the navel area... be 'very' careful not to tear off his manhood.

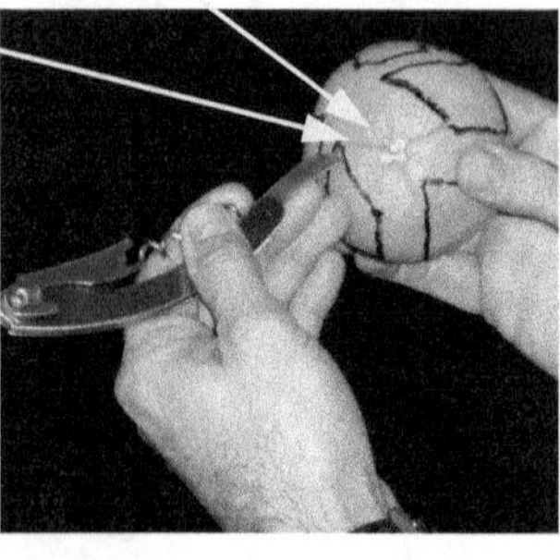

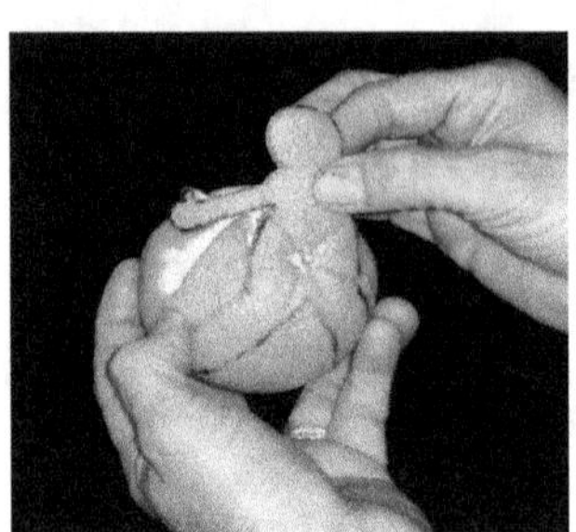

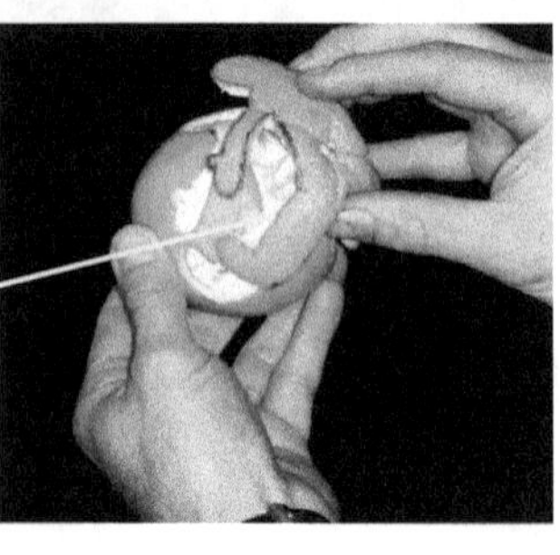

Agent Orange

Agent Orange is Happy To See You...

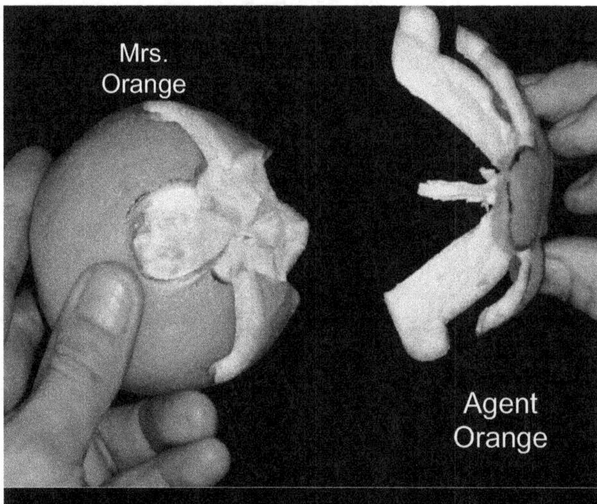

When you separate the two you will get a surprise. A very happy Agent Orange...

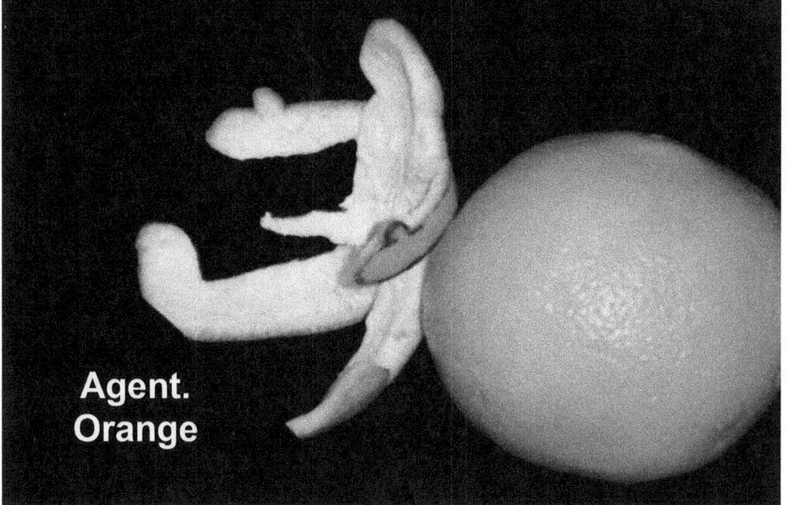

Champagne Chair

Here we are going to demonstrate how to make a Champagne Chair and Table.

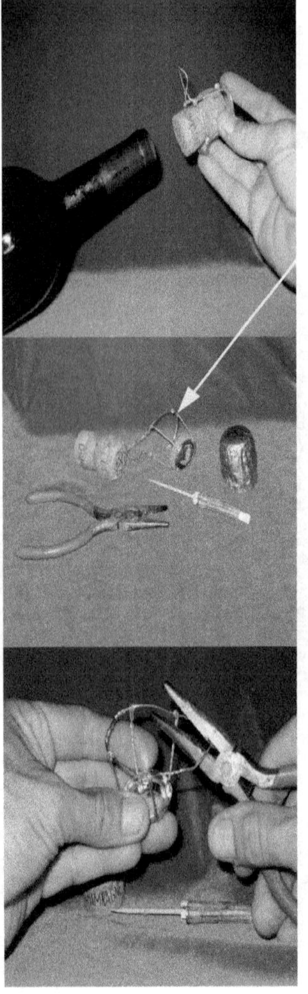

You will need a bottle of champagne. Complete with a cork, cage & foil.. Also a pair of pliers (with cutter) & a cocktail umbrella. Straighten the wire with the pliers, then cut it. The straighter the wire, the easier it is to pull the wire away from the seat base. It is important not to allow the 'seat' to pull away from the wire frame.

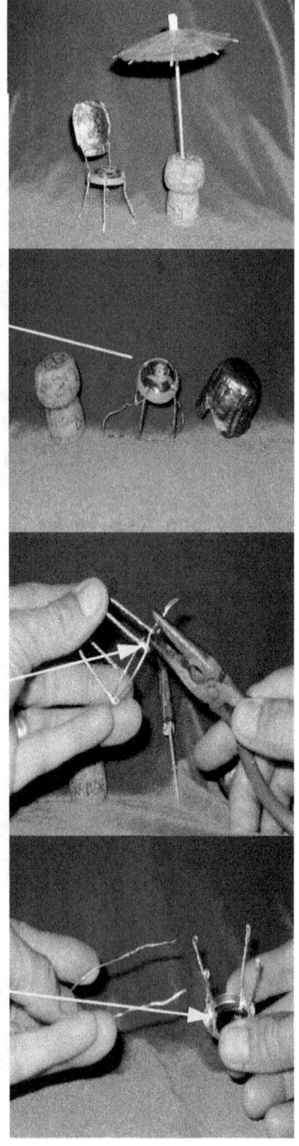

Champagne Chair

A crafty little ploy, that wins them over every time.

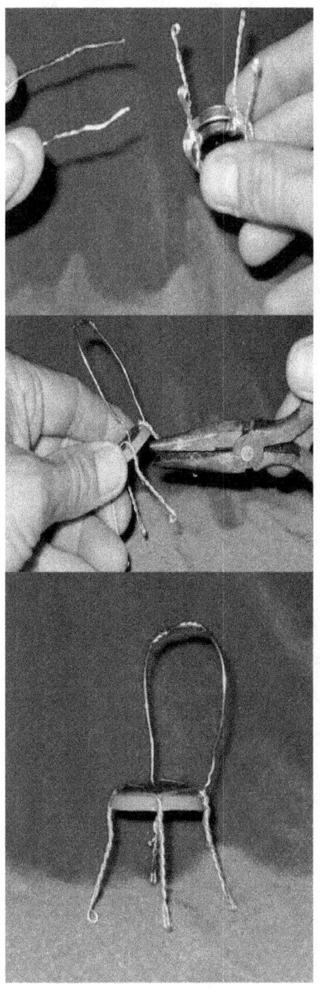

Okay... Spiral the wire 'with the grain' of the chair leg. Don't go down too far.

Now do the other side, & tighten them down with the pliers.

You're almost done! Tear the champagne foil into four panels, but don't tear them off. Refer to the next page.

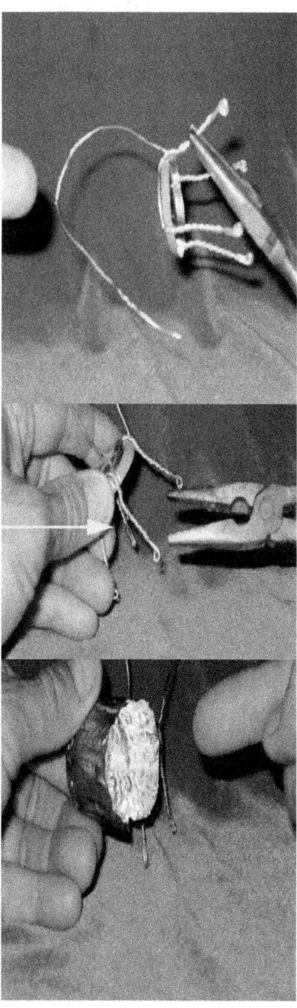

Champagne Chair

Tear right down through the middle of all four of them. 4 tears… 4 panels.

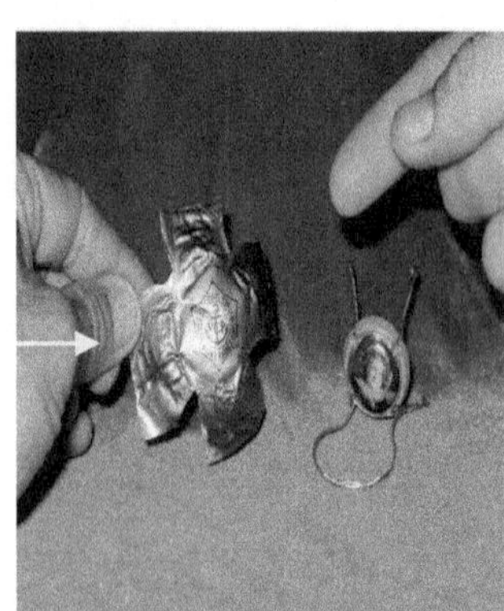

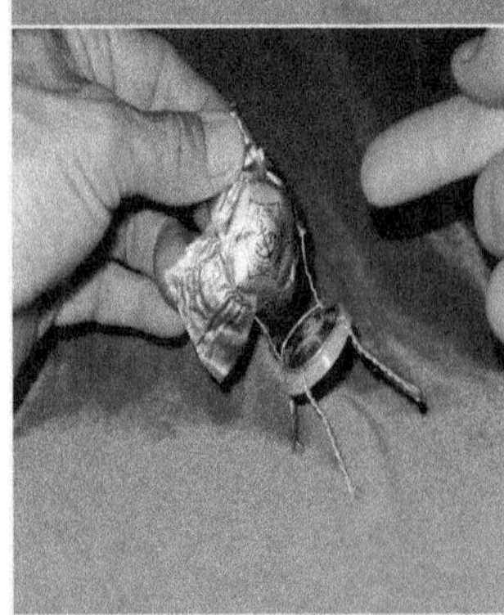

Wrap the 4 panels around the top of your chair. Be sure the logo is right side up.

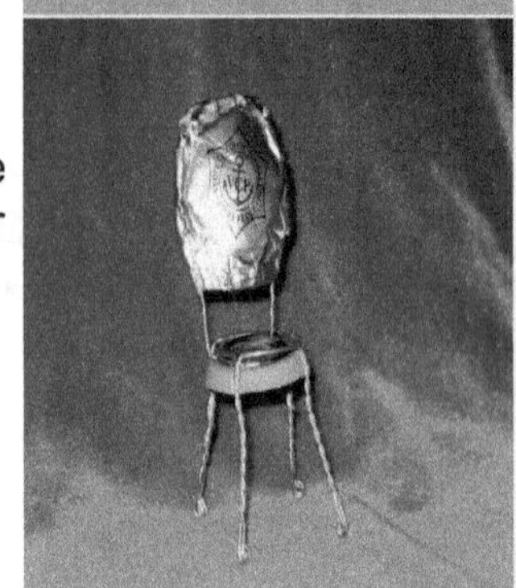

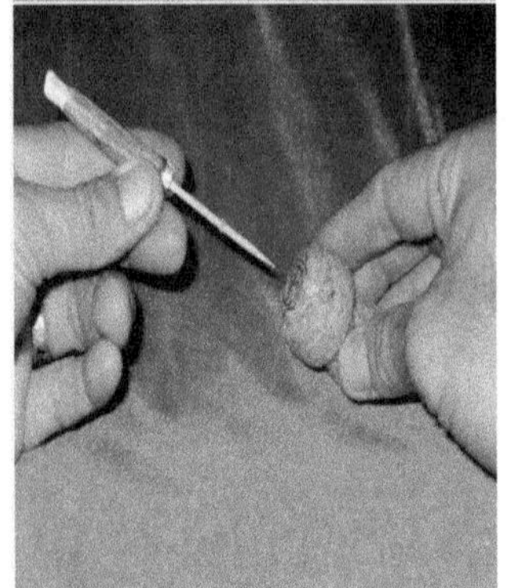

Here's your chair. Now put the umbrella in the cork, Gently.

Champagne Chair

Ta Da...!

"Keep this in a special place...
and come back for the rest of the set."

Sun To A Star

A 'SUN transforms into a 'STAR'
Right before your eyes...

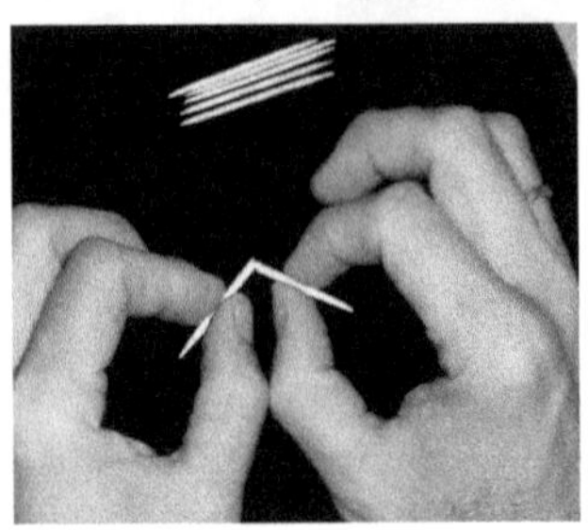

This is a cool one. You will need a beverage napkin, 5 wooden toothpicks, a glass of water & a hard dry surface. Take the toothpicks and 'crack' all of them in the middle. Don't 'break' them

through. Just crack 'em. Arrange them on the surface like this. Notice there are 5 of them.

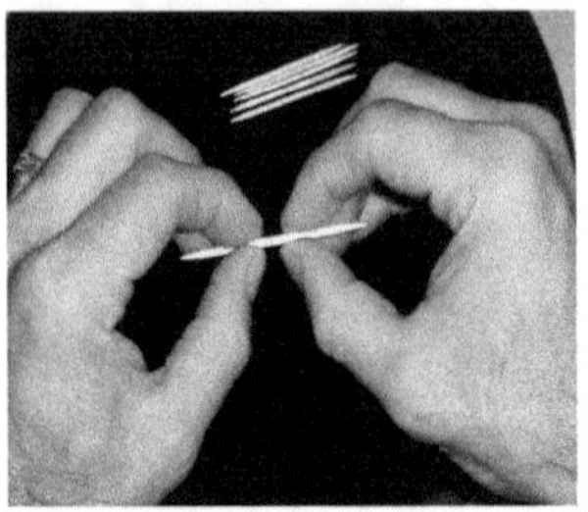

Sun To A Star

Amazing...

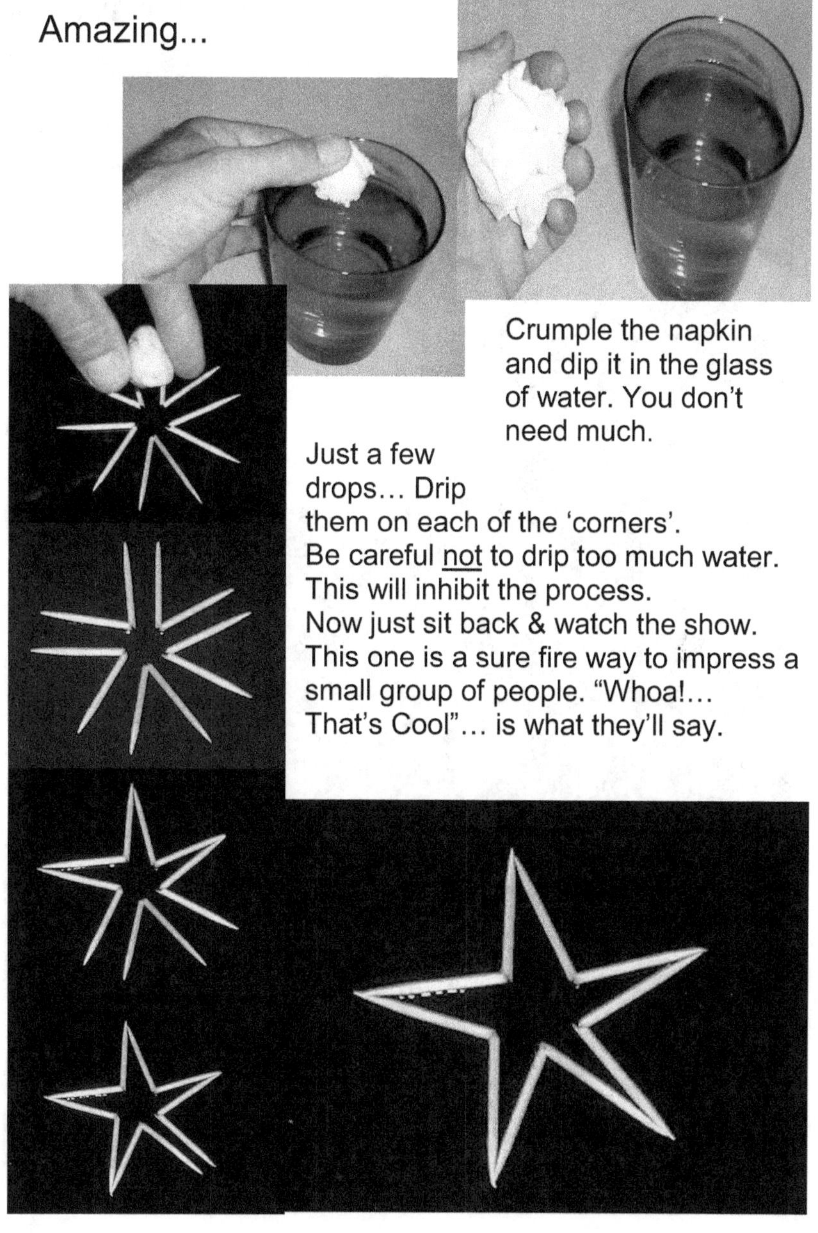

Crumple the napkin and dip it in the glass of water. You don't need much.

Just a few drops… Drip them on each of the 'corners'. Be careful not to drip too much water. This will inhibit the process. Now just sit back & watch the show. This one is a sure fire way to impress a small group of people. "Whoa!… That's Cool"… is what they'll say.

Bar Tricks are the perfect
'Ice-Breaker'

I have found that these
tricks create a certain
'playfulness' to the bar in
which I work.
My guests come back for
more. They can't get
enough!

The tricks outlined on the
preceding pages will amaze
and delight all your friends
and strangers alike.
Have fun with these.
Just 'Go For It'.

Chapter 8
Pick
Up
Lines

Okay So You Wanna Be Don Juan, huh?

What does it take to be successful at picking people up? Well… what does that mean exactly, anyway? Picking someone up? I'll pick you up for dinner? I'll pick you up for a movie? I'll pick you up by buying you a drink? Could I pick up the phone and call you later? Perhaps I could pick up the tab? Could I please pick up your skirt? Could I pick up your bath towel in the morning? Well… we gotta face it… this is really what we are talking about here, isn't it? How is it that I can get close to that gorgeous being over there. I'm out to meet someone… and now is the perfect time to act. So… go act. Be brave enough to walk over there and talk to that attractive person. You've got nothing to lose.

Don Who?

I'll just walk over there… Calmly look deeply into their eyes and say" ? ? ? ? " What? What do I say? Oh... now come the butterflies…

If I don't go over there and say something, I'll be kicking myself for not doing anything. If I go over there… I risk being laughed at or embarrassed. In a word… 'Shutdown.' Well… in all my wisdom and experience, all I can say is that this dilemma has faced mankind forever. We are no different from our forefathers… It seems they did it, why not you? Go on… Get out there. Try not to be shy. Go ahead and risk it. Go say, "Hello."

The downside is minimal! The upside? Well, you'll never know……….

if you don't try...

What Is a Good Pick Up Line?

So....What is a good pick up line?

One in which she smiles rather than rolls her eyes. It's in the timing, the delivery and the sincerity. By NOT saying anything, you are sure not to get noticed. There isn't any such thing as a perfect pick up line. Just one that gets you noticed rather than laughed at. Just say what's in your heart. Something like, "Hi... I'm ______. I noticed you when you got here and I felt compelled to ask you your name." Generally, here you would put out your hand to shake hers. She will say, "Hi, I'm ______." *(Smile)* Right now is your time to shine! Now you volley with... "Well miss, you are just as pretty up close, as you are from over there." Every girl likes to feel pretty! This is really the best one I've got...Sincerity! Just be yourself!

All you have to do is break the ice. The rest will follow. You cannot worry about looking like a fool, the fool is the one still back with his friends, talking smack...,

at least YOU are trying!

- My Mom is in town, staying at my place......................
  Could I stay at your place?

- Hey have we met?....No?...................
  Oh, excuse me.... It must have been this morning, right before I woke up!

- If it's true you are what you eat, ...
  Then I could be you by morning!

- I'm writing a telephone book...
  Could I have your number?

- Hi!....I'm Mr. Right.............................
  I heard you've been looking for me.

- Do you sleep on your tummy at night?...... Can I?

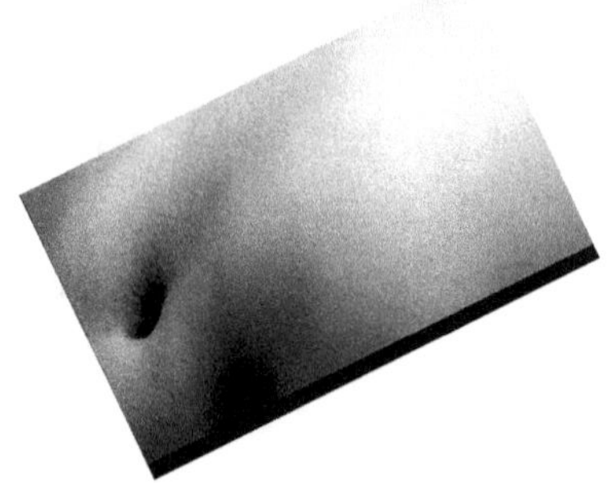

- Do you have any overdue library books at your house?.................. You have FINE written all over you.

- Is that a ladder in your stockings?........... .... or the stairway to heaven?

- If I told you that you had a beautiful body, ...would you hold it against me?

- You've got 206 bones in your body................... ....Want one more?

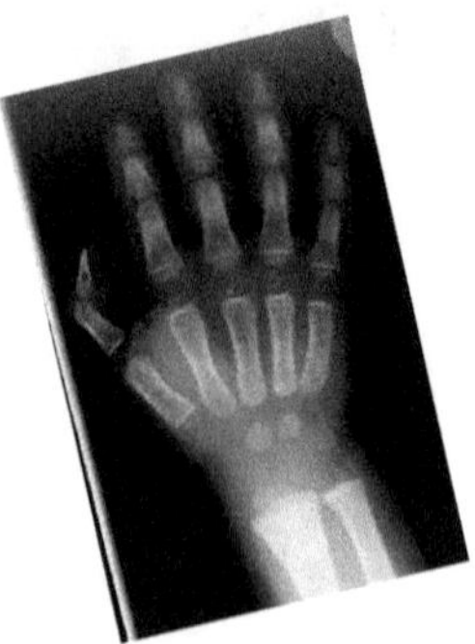

- Excuse me, I'm an ornithologist and I've been looking for the pink breasted bed thrasher. ....Have you seen one?

- Nice shirt... What do you think it would look like on my floor?

- Wanna come over for some pizza and sex? ...."What....you don't like pizza?"

- Are you from Tennessee?
  You're the only ten I see!

- I forgot my phone number....... Could I have yours?....

- We would have beautiful children together.

- If I could change the alphabet, I would put you and I together...

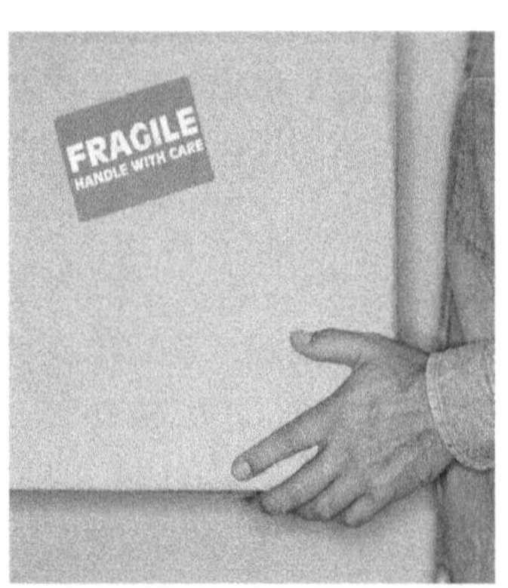

- Do you work for UPS? .... I thought you were checking out my package.

- Do you believe in love at first sight?
  Or should I walk by again?

- Nice Shoes.............. Wanna go home with me?"

- You look like my first wife…
  And I've never been married.

- You must be tired……………………………
  From running around my mind all day…

- How long will they let you stay?
  You must be sent here to earth by the heavens to show us mortals true beauty.

- ...Lick your finger and wipe it on her shirt...
  and then say……………………
  "Lets get you out of these wet clothes."

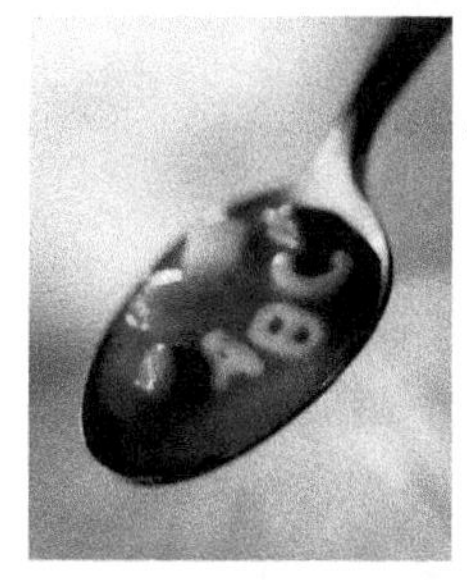

- Do you work for Campbell Soup?……………………………
  Cause your Mm Mm Good

- Hi...I'm new in town, and I'd really like to know how to get to your place….

- If your left leg was Thanksgiving and your right leg was Christmas............................ ...could I visit you between the holidays?

- I have something in my eye........ YOU!

- Hey, excuse me......................................
"Are you single?"

- I hate to see you go, but it's nice to watch you walk away.

- You can feel the magic between us............ ...No... lower......

- How would you like to wake up, and go to work in those clothes tomorrow morning?

- Where have you been
  all these beers…?

- Are you OK?
  Maybe you should be home in bed?
  ....Here are my keys.

- You better get used to me… We could be together until after breakfast.

- I don't hate you because you're beautiful.

- Is that a mirror in your pocket?
  I think I can see myself in your pants.

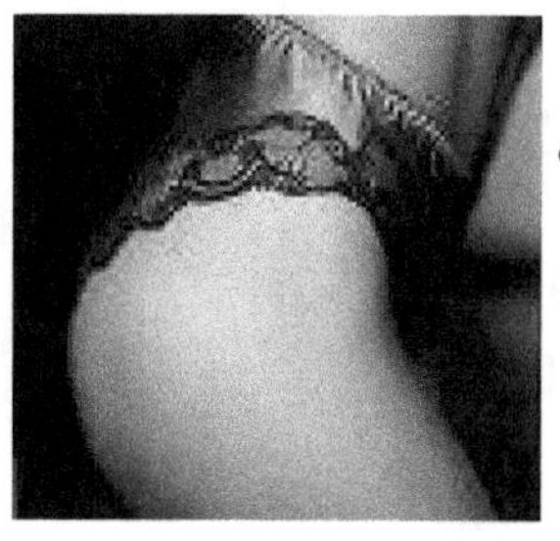

- Didn't I see you in a
  Victoria's Secret
  Catalog?

- Check the tag on her shirt or jacket, then say… “Yep!... I knew it, ...made in heaven!”

- Wanna play army?……….
  I’ll lay down……….
  and you swoop in
  and blow the hell out
  of me.

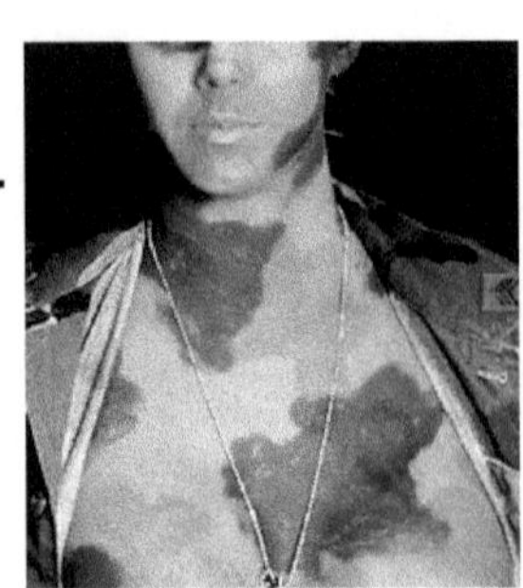

- I’d love to see how you look when I’m naked…

- Nice Legs………………………………………
  Can I take you shopping for some shoes?

- Drop a packet of sugar in front of your quest… and say… “I think you dropped your name tag.”

- Could I borrow your phone?......................
  My Mom told me to call
  when I met the perfect girl...

- I'd walk a mile through a hungry lion's den in pork chop underwear……………….. ……... just to see you smile!

- Did it Hurt?
  When you fell
  from heaven?

- "You look beautiful!"
  You could always use the direct and honest approach...

- Your eyes are as deep as the ocean……… Save me I'm drowning.

- Is that a fox on your shoulder or am I seeing double?

- Shhhhh! You may be asked to leave soon.... The other ladies here are starting to resent your beauty... But I can escort you out safely.

- I've heard milk does a body good,.......
  but ***damn***, how much have you been drinking?

- "Hi!...I'm Rich,..........
  .... but you should see me naked!"

- I'm not supposed to eat three hours before bedtime..........But I could make an exception in your case....

- I'm an organ donor.......
  .... Need anything?

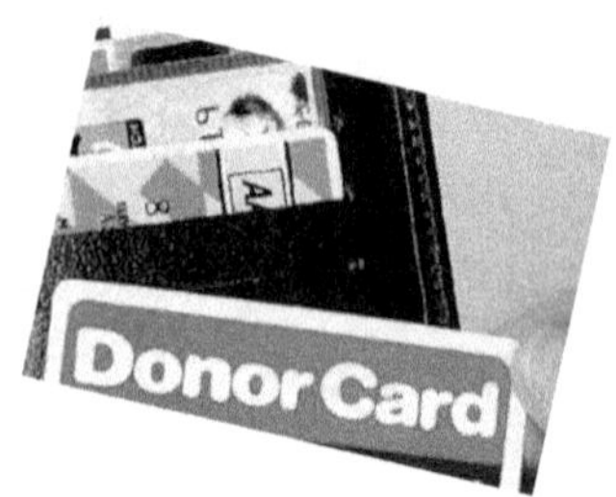

- I'm having a dream tonight...................... Wanna come over and be in it?

- Are your parents terrorists?... Cause you're the bomb!

- Is your shirt Braille? I read Braille and I sense you have a message for me. (this one is handy for a logo shirt)

- I didn't know angels could fly so low...

- I lost my puppy, can you help me find him?............... ....I think he went into that motel across the street.

Chapter 9
Liquid
Measures
&
Conversions

1 Case Wine	~ 50 Glasses	50 Glasses	12 Bottles		305 ounces
1 Case Champagne	~ 60 Flutes	60 Glasses	12 Bottles		305 ounces
1 Wine Vine	~ 3 Bottles	12 Glasses			
1 Barrel Wine	60 Gallons	20 Cases	~ 1000 Glasses		
1 Bottle Wine	750 ml	4 Glasses	25.4 oz.	750 ml	
1/4 gallon	1 quart	2 pints	4 cups	32 ounces	
1/2 quart	1 pint	2 cups	8 oz.	16 ounces	
1 gallon	4 quarts	8 pints	16 cups	128 ounces	
1/2 gallon	2 quarts	4 pints	8 cups	64 ounces	
1/4 gallon	1 quart	2 pints	4 cups	32 ounces	
1 quart	2 pints	4 cups	.95 liter	32 ounces	
1/2 quart	1 pint	2 cups	.47 liter	16 ounces	

1 Cup	8 oz.		236 ml	
½ cup	4 oz			
1/4 cup	2 ounces			
1/8 cup	1 ounce			
1 dram	1/8 ounce	3.7 ml		
1/8 cup	1 ounce	29.6 ml		
1 Liter	1000 ml	33.6 ounces		
Half Bottle	375 ml		2 glasses	
Split Bottle	187 ml		1 glass	
Magnum	1.5 Bottle Wine			
Double Mag	3 Bottles of Wine			
Jeroboam	4 Bottles of Wine			
Methuselah	8 Bottles of Wine			
Salmanzanar	12 Bottles of Wine			
1 Keg Beer	1984 ounces of Beer	156 '12 oz' Beers	124 '16oz' Beers	

Chapter 10
Glossary
of Terms

ABC—Alcohol Bureau of Control

ABV—The measurement for alcoholic strength of a spirit. The ABV is measured as a percentage part of the entire liquid. For example an ABV of 30%, is 30% alcohol 70% water.

Anejo—Tequila which has been aged for over a year.

Agave—A plant that looks like a cactus used in the production of Tequila and Mezcal.

Age Statement—The age on a bottle which refers to the age of the youngest ingredient.

Angel's Share—The phrase used for the amount of spirit which evaporates during the distillation process.

Bar Spoon—A long handled spoon used to stir cocktails. These spoons often come with a spiraled handle to help twirl the spoon

Beading—The method of assessing a spirit's strength by shaking the bottle to produce bubbles, (beads). The larger the bubbles and the longer they last the stronger the spirit.

Bitters—An extract made from fruits, herbs and roots often added to a cocktail to help flavor it.

Black Label—Johnnie Walker ® "Black Label."

Blending—The mixing of different types of spirit or the mixing of different ages of the same spirit.

Boilermaker—Originally was "a shot-and-a-beer," meaning a shot of whiskey followed by a beer chaser. Sometimes known as a "drop shot."

Boston Shaker—Large cup shaped shaker tin, used to help shake cocktails before they are served. They come in two halves with the metal half placed over a mixing glass in order to shake the drink. To be then "strained" into the serving glass with a strainer.

Boston Tin—A metal shaker used to mix cocktails, that covers a mixing glass in order to shake them both together.

Botanicals—Herbs, peel, flowers, etc. used to flavor spirits like junipers in gin.

Bouilleur—French name for a distiller.

Brandewijn—Dutch name for grape spirit which is now brandy.

Bruising—Bruising or "to bruise" an ingredient often refers to when a drink is shaken and the alcohol is more violently mixed. It is argued the gin can be bruised as it is made from juniper berries, leading to a cloudy appearance and altered taste in the finished drink.

Caipirinha—A muddled lime and sugar cocktail, made with only with Cachaça Rum from Brazil. This is the national drink of Brazil.

Caiparisima—A cocktail made with premium rum from the Islands, but not necessarily 'Cachaça Rum', from Brazil..
A muddled lime and sugar drink.

Caiparoska—Made with premium Vodka from the Vodklan Islands. Just kidding. It's the same drink as a caipirinha except with Vodka.

Caiparisma—Same drink… with Gin.

Camper—The term used by restaurant and bar employees to describe a patron who buys one drink and nurses it for hours. Taking up a bar stool, but not buying drinks or tipping.

Cask Strength—The term for a spirit which has been mixed with water to reduce its strength to the standard strength.

Chimney Shaker—A silver or silver plated martini shaker with a lid and a strainer built into the lid. No shaker glass needed.

Chaser—A mixer that is tossed down the gullet after one has drunk a straight shot of whiskey or other spirit instead of being combined with a spirit in a glass.

Cola Back— Means that the guest wants to have a short cola on the side of a straight liquor. "A shot and a cola."

Cold Compounding— The term for the method of adding concentrated flavors to neutral spirits. This is method of adding flavor is cheaper then infusion but gives a rougher end product.

Collins— Basically a sour in a tall glass with club soda or seltzer water. The famous Tom Collins made with gin has been extended to include everything from applejack, (*a Jack Collins*), to Irish whiskey, (*Mike Collins*), or (*John Collins),* which is made with vodka.

Collins Glass— A tall glass tumbler used to serve a mixed drink. The glass usually holds 10—14 ounces.

Congeners— Chemical compounds produced during the fermentation, distillation and maturing process. These compounds contain a lot of the flavor in a spirit and the fewer amount of congeners the stronger the spirit is.

Cooler—An iced drink made with wine, usually red, perhaps a liqueur, or any fruit juice, sometimes with a splash of soda water or ginger ale. A Sangria is a loosely fitting description of what a cooler is.

Distillation— The method of using heat to extract alcohol from fermented liquid. Due to alcohol boiling at a lower temperature then water the vapor given off can be condensed making the spirit stronger.

Dram— The term for a glass of a certain spirit used most commonly in Scotland, Ireland and Jamaica.

Eau-de-Vie— The French name for brandy and other spirits made from fruit.

Eggnog— A traditional Christmas holiday bowl containing a delectable combination of eggs, sugar, cream or milk, and brandy, rum, or bourbon served cold in individual cups in all it's rich. creamy goodness.

Fizz— There are many fine old recipes for Fizzes, which are as the name suggests, products of the old siphon bottle that "fizzed" the drink with a stream of bubbles as it was being made. The Gin Fizz is typical and similar to the Tom Collins.

Flip— A creamy, cold drink made of eggs, sugar, and your favorite wine or spirit. The Brandy Flip and the Sherry Flip are perhaps best known. The Flip began in Colonial times as a hot drink made of spirits, beer, eggs, cream, and spices, sometimes it was 'mulled' with a red-hot flip iron.

Grog—Originally a mixture of rum and water that was issued to sailors in the Royal Navy and later improved with the addition of lime juice and sugar. Now a Grog is any kind of drink, usually made with a rum base, fruit, and various sweeteners, and served either hot or cold in a large mug or glass. Reputedly named after Admiral Edward Vernon, who was called "Old Grog" because of the grogram cape he wore.

Hawthorn Strainer— A strainer with a wire spring designed to fit over the top of the stainless steel half of a Boston Shaker.

Highball— Any spirit served with ice in a tall glass. Various mixers may be used.

Highball Glass— A glass used to serve cocktails, 'tall' around 10—14 ounces.

Holandas— Spanish Brandy

Infusion—Method of extracting flavor from ingredients by marinating them together. For example… fresh fruit may be used to 'infuse' it's flavor into vodka, by cutting the fruit up and 'marinating' it in a bath of vodka. In 36 hours, the vodka will taste like fruit and the fruit will taste like vodka. Presto…

Jack Black— Jack Daniel's ® 'Black Label'.

Julep— A venerable drink made of Kentucky bourbon, sugar, mint leaves, and plenty of crushed ice. An American classic.

Lip Space— Small space left at the top of a glass often to avoid spillage.

Lowball—A short drink consisting of spirits served with ice alone, or with water or soda in a short bucket glass.

Mist—A glass packed with crushed ice to which spirits are added, usually straight.

Mouth Feel—The texture of a drink when being tasted.

Muddle— Mixing, smashing & blending ingredients via pressing & stirring them in a glass. Done using a muddler.

Mulled— Wine or wine drinks that are heated and served as hot punches. Also called mulled wine from the time when drinks were heated with a red-hot poker, loggerhead, or flip iron.

Neat— A straight shot of any spirit in a glass without any accompaniment or ice.

Negus—A hot, sweet drink, with or without spices. Port or sherry traditional. Named after colonel Francis Negus, an eighteenth-century English luminary.

Neutral Alcohol— A spirit above 95.5% which also contains few or no congeners.

Nose—The aroma of a drink or wine.

Nightcap— Any drink that is taken immediately before retiring. Milk punches, toddies, and short drinks such as liqueurs or fortified wines are favored.

On-the-Rocks— Any wine or spirit poured over ice cubes, usually in Old Fashioned glass.

Overproof—High strength, un-aged rum.

Paille—French rum aged for less then 3 years.

Pick-Me-Up— Any concoction designed to allay the effects of overindulgence in alcoholic beverages.

Puff— A combination of spirits and milk mixed in equal parts and topped with club soda. Usually served in an Old Fashioned glass.

Punch— A combination of spirits, wine, sweeteners, flavorings, fruit garnishes, and sometimes various carbonated beverages mixed in and served from a large bowl to a number of people. Individually made punches are called

Press— A mixed drink, usually vodka or gin, but often whiskey, served with half soda water and half lemon lime soda.. This makes the drink a little less sweet..

Proof—The American term for ABV, 100 proof is 50% ABV

Reposado— Tequila aged 'on oak' from three months to a year.

Repo— Short for Reposado.

Rickey— A drink made with gin or other spirit, lime juice, and club soda, usually served with ice in a small highball or Rickey glass, with or without sweetening. Named for Colonel Joe Rickey, and old-time Washingtonian

Rocks— As in served over the rocks or 'Ice Cubes'.

Sangaree—A tall drink containing chilled spirits, wine, or beer, sometimes sweetened and given a good dusting with grated nutmeg.

Shooter—Taken neat, as a single 'throwback'.

Shrub—Spirits, fruit juices, and sugar, aged in a sealed container such as a cask or crock, then usually bottled.

Sling—A tall drink made with lemon juice, sugar, and spirits, usually served cold with club soda.

Slurp—To 'have just a touch more'...
"Please Mr. Bartender... just a slurp".
My dear friend Ramon Martin used to say this. RIP Ray...

Splash—Just a little bit, as in about a half ounce or less.

Smash—A short muddled cocktail, made of spirits, sugar, and fresh herbs, usually served in an Old Fashioned glass.

Sour—A short drink made or lemon or lime juice, sugar, and spirits. The whiskey Sour is the classic Sour, but may be made with vodka, gin, rum, brandy, or various liqueurs, especially fruit-flavored cordials such as apricot or peach.

Swizzle— Originally a tall rum cooler filled with cracked ice that was swizzled with a long twig, stirring rod or spoon rotated rapidly between the palms of the hands to produce frost on the glass. The Swizzle, a Caribbean invention, is made with any kind of spirit today and is traditionally served in a tall highball or collins glass.

Syllabub— An old English recipe consisting of milk, cream, sugar, and spices, blended with sherry, port, or Madeira to produce a very sweet, creamy mixture that is often served in a sherbet glass as a dessert.

Three Amigos— Tequila, triple sec & sweet & sour or fresh squeezed lime juice. With Sweet & Sour it's an Americano style, with lime juice is more traditional Mexican style.

Toddy— Originally a hot drink made with spirits, sugar, spices, and a lemon peel mixed with hot water and served in a tall glass. A toddy may be served cold with ice, and any combination of spices and spirits, but is usually served hot.

Tot— A small amount of any beverage, a short shot, or a touch.

UP— Usually a martini or specific gin or vodka served UP or in a martini glass.

VS—Very Special

VSOP—Very Special Old Pale—Aged

White Label—Dewar's® 'White Label' Scotch

XO—Extra Old—The French name for top quality spirits which have been aged for 6 to 7 years minimum.

Be Safe...
Call A Cab!

This book is NOT intended to promote drinking. It has been written to be a starting point towards entertaining your guests. This guide is intended to be an informative and entertaining look into the modern day, high volume bartender's world. As a last word, it is important to remember that it is the responsibility of the host to look after their guests. While they are at the gathering and beyond.

We emphatically encourage our readers to enjoy these and all spirited beverages responsibly and in moderation.
Be aware and don't let anyone drive drunk.
If you know about it,
you can do something about it.
Put a stop to it! Please be careful!

Do the right thing...
Don't Drink & Drive...
Call A Cab!

Blake F. Donaldson

is the self proclaimed...

guardian of the 'art of bartending'.

Voted Bartender of the Year locally and acclaimed nationally.

Los Angeles Magazine called him 'Mr. Martini'.

He has defined and illustrated for us here, the **Basics of Bartending** and the main **Cocktail Recipes** of today. All designed to show the perspective entertainer or devoted bartender some tools to work with to dazzle your friends and guests. You don't have to be an expert...just sincere.

"Have fun with this stuff..." Blake

www.ingramcontent.com/pod-product-compliance
Lightning Source LLC
LaVergne TN
LVHW051501080426
835509LV00017B/1865

9780974505947